ORIENTAL RUG PRIMER

ORIENTAL
RUG
PRIMER

BUYING AND UNDERSTANDING NEW ORIENTAL RUGS

BY

ARAM K. JERREHIAN, JR.

RUNNING PRESS
PHILADELPHIA, PENNSYLVANIA

Canadian representatives: General Publishing,
30 Lesmill Road, Don Mills, Ontario M3B2T6

9   8   7   6
Digit on the right indicates the number of this printing.

LIBRARY OF CONGRESS CATALOGING IN PUBLICATION DATA

Jerrehian, Aram K., Jr.,1934–
Oriental Rug Primer

Bibliography: p. 206
Includes Index
1.   Rugs, Oriental—Handbooks, manuals, etc.
I. Title.
NK2808.J47   747.7'5   79–19724
ISBN 0–89471–077–X paperback
ISBN 0–89471–078–8 library binding

COVER PHOTOGRAPH: *Basmakci* (Turkey)

Cover art direction by James Wizard Wilson
Color photography by Michael LaRiche
Interior illustration by Suzanne Clee

Typography: Paladium, with Garamond, by rci, Philadelphia, Pennsylvania
Printed in Hong Kong by Leefung–Asco Ltd.

This book may be ordered directly from the publisher.
Please include $1.00 postage.

Try your bookstore first.

Running Press
125 South Twenty-Second Street
Philadelphia, Pennsylvania 19103

IN MEMORY OF
CHRISTOPHER H. PEROT
—Would I forget you?

CONTENTS

ACKNOWLEDGMENTS

When I began work on this book, I had no idea that the efforts of so many people would be involved. I'm particularly grateful to: Amatulli Imports, Inc., Davis & Nahikian, Fritz & LaRue Company, Karim Rug Corporation, Leo's International Trade, N. Levian Rug Company, A. Morjikian, and Noonoo Rug Company, for rugs; Albert Amini, Richard Amatulli, Haig Asaduorian, Archie A. Cherkezian, and Paul Vesley, for information; John L. Akard, for research; Melissa Shuwall and Jackie Millett, for typing; Alida Becker, for editing; Peter John Dorman, for design; Larry and Stuart Teacher, for asking; and, finally, to my family, Jackie, Amy, Dean, and Ellen, for persevering.

A.K.J.

LIST OF COLOR PLATES

(following page 32)

ORIENTAL RUG PRIMER

INTRODUCTION

WHEN YOU'RE BUYING AN ORIENTAL RUG FOR THE FIRST TIME YOU'RE likely to be a bit intimidated by the mystique of the world you're about to enter. You may have seen fine Oriental rugs in museums, leafed through expensive and lavishly illustrated books on the subject, and read an article or two about the advantages of "investing" in an Oriental rug. You may even have heard a few stories about a dirty old rug found in an attic that turned out to be worth thousands—or a rug bought at auction for thousands that turned out to be worthless. It's not surprising, then, that picking out your first Oriental rug can seem like working your way through a mine field—you want to make the right choice, and at the same time you want to keep from making costly mistakes. And so you feel, quite rightly, that you're in need of expert advice.

Until very recently, Oriental rugs have been considered the exclusive territory of a relatively small group of collectors, dealers, and aficionados, but within the past few years the tide has turned. Not surprisingly, a host of books on Oriental rugs has also appeared—and the first-time buyer usually starts out with one of them. A number of these books are excellent, scholarly works, lavishly illustrated and obviously the result of careful, in-depth research. Naturally, they feature the finest examples of the art of rugmaking. However, while you can certainly admire these masterpieces, there's little hope that you can ever actually own one. The closest you're likely to get is a do-not-touch, long-distance look at a museum.

A number of less sophisticated but well-intentioned books have also appeared in the past few years, but all too many of their illustrations appear to have been chosen simply because certain rugs were handy, readily available to be photographed. The question of whether the rugs are attractive and of good quality doesn't seem to have been seriously considered. Still other books, written by individual collectors, may contain interesting rugs, but their primary purpose seems to lie in documenting the author's own collection.

Almost all of these books share the same shortcoming—they place too much emphasis on the process of identifying various types of Oriental rugs. While no one would argue that this isn't a valuable basic skill, it's also true that concentrating on names and types can often lead to a good deal of frustration when you're actually trying to buy a rug. If you start off this way, you can easily become sidetracked and lose sight of the main consideration in buying an Oriental—satisfying your own personal taste. After all, Oriental rugs are handcrafted works of art, and works of art are meant to be enjoyed. If you begin simply by seeing and handling dozens of rugs—without worrying too much about what they are and where they come from—you can appreciate their beauty and get a feeling for the colors and designs that please you. Only then should you move on to assessing the details of type and quality.

Another misconception that's fostered by many books on Oriental rugs is the notion that an antique or semi-antique Oriental is the only kind that's worth considering. Even if this were true (and of course it isn't), the fact of the matter is that older rugs that are in good condition have become quite rare and extremely expensive—and older rugs that are damaged or have been repaired can be almost as costly. It's obvious, then, that buying and selling older rugs can be a risky proposition unless you know exactly what you're doing, and with whom you're dealing.

But this doesn't mean that you have to give up. Handmade Orientals continue to be produced throughout the world, and new

Introduction

Orientals have always outsold older pieces many times over. Contrary to what's often believed, today's rugs can be of the finest quality, and even those of average quality can often be better buys than threadbare, worn, or raveled older rugs.

There are a number of other advantages in buying a new Oriental. Present-day weavers are more flexible in meeting the needs of the world-wide rug market, and they've responded to changes in demand by producing classic designs in a greater range of qualities, sizes, and colors. This also means that there's more standardization in modern rug production than in the past—which can actually be a positive factor for the novice. After all, if there's stricter regulation of the weaving process then it's easier for you to concentrate on the one determination that only you can make—finding a rug that you like.

This isn't to say, of course, that you don't need *some* knowledge of rugs before you buy a new Oriental. You need to be able to understand the precepts of traditional rugmaking and apply them to the contemporary scene—to discover which rugs are being made in reasonable quantities and qualities, what adaptations have been made in designs and colors, and what all this means in terms of your own financial and practical situation. That's where the *Oriental Rug Primer* comes in.

If you're tempted to look at the photographs (assuming that you haven't already done so), go right ahead—they're the heart of this book. By paging through the color portfolio, you'll start to get a feeling for the color and design combinations that appeal to you. You'll also see a fair representation of the kinds of rugs that are being produced for the American market, the kinds of rugs that should reasonably be available here. These rugs were carefully chosen to represent the selection you're likely to find in your local rug shops. All are of average or better quality. Some are available in many colors, others in a limited selection. All their patterns, whether simple or ornate, are in keeping with the traditional designs of the past.

Of course, you may not be able to exactly duplicate the rugs you see in this book—it would take tens of thousands of illustrations to show every rug that's made today. However, in many cases they'd only be variations of the rugs found in the color section of this primer. On the other hand, there's no reason to avoid buying a certain kind of rug simply because you've seen very similar rugs in a number of shops. Remember, the Oriental rug market is still comparatively small and exclusive—there's very little chance that you'll see a rug just like yours in your neighbor's living room.

Once you've browsed through the photographs, return to the text. Here you'll find all the information you'll need to make an intelligent—and painless—purchase. You'll learn how to evaluate the quality of a rug and—of equal importance—have a realization of just what's involved in the craft of rug weaving. Knowing how a rug is made will give you an appreciation of its cost and value, and will allow you to consider these factors in terms of your own needs.

Naturally, each major weaving area has its own particular specialties and idiosyncracies, and you'll also learn about them here. In addition, the directory of rug types will help you to become familiar with the most common terms used to identify particular groups of rugs, and the cross-referencing system will help you find other groups that are similar. A supplemental listing at the end of the directory will help you track down less common types, and the glossary will answer your questions about any other terms you might encounter.

You'll also learn where to buy rugs and where not to buy them, as well as when to buy them. You'll be given step-by-step pointers on inspecting a rug, and the section for shopping notes at the back of the book will help you keep track of what you've seen and where, to get the most out of your comparison shopping. In addition, the Appendix provides you with detailed instructions on scaling your rooms and your furniture arrangements so you can realistically assess your needs and your options. Once you've gotten your rug home (or have one home on trial) you'll learn how to use it in your decorating scheme and how to take proper care of it. And, if you should be so inclined, you'll also learn how to resell your rug or trade up.

Throughout the book, historical descriptions have been kept

Introduction

to a minimum. In my opinion, this kind of knowledge isn't essential to the novice, nor is it necessary for you to understand the symbolism of the various designs. Once you've bought a rug or two, you might like to read up on antique rugs and learn some of the fine points of the traditional rug designs. If so, you'll find recommendations for further reading in the Bibliography.

However, in the beginning you shouldn't attempt to turn yourself into an expert. Trying to sort out all the scholarly details of designs and histories when you're picking out your first rug can lead to a lot of confusion—and you may be teaching yourself myths instead of realities. Remember, you're buying a rug, not a story. Oriental rugs may have a past that's filled with romance, but you should never be romanced into making a purchase.

I've chosen to call this book the *Oriental Rug Primer* because I see myself not as a scholar of Oriental rugs, but as a teacher dedicated to passing along what I've learned of the art and craft of rugmaking. By reading the book carefully, you'll be able to find answers to all the questions asked by novice rug buyers—and to discover other areas you can explore as you become more familiar with the particular kinds of rugs you like and with Oriental rugs in general.

Although the *Oriental Rug Primer* wasn't written for specialists, I believe that anyone who cares about Oriental rugs will find much that's of interest here. In particular, it's my hope that this little book will smooth the way for both the buyer and the seller of Oriental rugs. As a dealer, I know all too well how much confusion and wasted energy can be involved in the purchase of an Oriental rug—and I know that it doesn't have to be that way. The *Oriental Rug Primer* will give you the basic information I wish all my customers had when they first came into my establishment. And, of equal importance, it will allow you to enjoy to the fullest the experience of buying and owning an Oriental rug.

—Aram K. Jerrehian, Jr.
WYNNEWOOD, PENNSYLVANIA, 1980

CHAPTER I

WHAT IS AN ORIENTAL RUG?

IN A GENERAL SENSE, AN ORIENTAL RUG CAN be defined as any rug made in a broad geographical area that stretches from the Atlantic Ocean to the Pacific. To the east, this region encompasses the "Orient" as it's known to Europeans, and to the west it extends to the limits of the old Moorish empire. True Oriental rugs also have in common the manner in which they're made—and in the final analysis this may be the only similarity among them.

Oriental rugs are either flat-woven or hand-knotted. In flat-woven, pileless rugs, a crosshatch of horizontal and vertical threads forms both the fabric of the rug and the basis for its design. In hand-knotted rugs, the flat-woven fabric is given an added dimension when strands of yarn are tied, or looped, into the foundation. The cut ends of these knots form the pile of the rug and create its pattern.

In the past, a distinction was also made between "rugs" and "carpets." The former were smaller, and the latter were large enough to cover the entire floor of a room. These days, however, the terms are to all intents and purposes indistinguishable, and they'll be used interchangeably in the pages that follow.

21

A Brief History

It's difficult to explore the precise origins of rug weaving, not only because of the small number of remnants that have survived, but also because of the scarcity of historical records in some of the areas in which weaving was likely to have begun. It's generally agreed that weaving as we know it was done in Egypt and Central Asia well before it took hold in Persia, the country most people associate with Oriental rugs.

The earliest pile fabrics have been discovered by archaeologists in Egyptian tombs. These are looped pieces, made of linen, and they seem to have been used as clothing and hangings, but definitely not as rugs. The earliest known pile rug was found by Russian archaeologists in a Scythian burial site in Outer Mongolia. This most interesting artifact, which had been frozen after grave robbers damaged the tomb, has been dated to the fifth century B.C. It's a surprisingly skillful and sophisticated piece of work that bears a striking resemblance to some of the finest modern carpets.

These discoveries, and others throughout Turkey, Egypt, and Central Asia (to name just a few), give us tantalizing hints of what the fragile textiles of the past may have been like. For the most part, however, evidence of the existence of carpets and woven fabrics must come from the records provided by paintings, murals, ceramics, and carvings, as well as descriptions contained in the literature that's been passed down to us through the ages.

There's little consistency in terms of quality and design among the oldest rugs that are still in existence today. Many early pieces are quite sophisticated, while others are strictly utilitarian. Nevertheless, the techniques of construction must have had to develop in steps and stages, and this process probably occurred independently in various parts of the world.

Rug weaving undoubtedly began with nomadic weavers, members of tribes that ranged across cold, windy lands and bred sheep not only for meat but for wool. They used primitive looms to produce flat fabrics, and in the earliest days these rugs probably had no patterns at all. Soon, though, it was discovered that different-colored horizontal threads could produce simple patterns using the grey or brown tones of the natural wool. Gradually, the designs of these early rugs became more elaborate and colorful as the weavers discovered how to create a range of dyes from the plants and animals around them. This basic two-dimensional weaving technique, using only horizontal and vertical threads in predominantly geometrical patterns, results in a flat rug called a kilim. From the earliest times to the present day, rugs have been produced using only this simple means of construction.

The nomadic weavers produced more than kilims, however. The next step was to add a third dimension to the flat rug through the introduction of pile, the twisting of tufts of wool around the threads of the fabric to create a deeper, warmer material. After this, a shortcut was discovered in which the knots were inserted while the basic fabric was woven.

These weaving techniques spread from the nomadic tribes into the villages, and as the centuries passed they took hold throughout the Orient. Then, in the seventh century, a further development came with the rise of Islam. As it became the dominant force in the Arab world, the teaching of the Prophet had a tremendous impact on the designs used in the weaving of the Near East. It was also the force that brought carpetmaking to even more areas of the world. At its height, the Arab empire stretched from Spain to India, and it was contact with this empire that helped introduce the Oriental rug to Europe.

Until the close of the Middle Ages, Europeans covered their floors with loose rushes or rush mats. Tapestries were hung on walls for decoration and to block chilly drafts; they were much too valuable to be placed on the floor. The first pile carpets were brought to Europe from the Ottoman Empire by Italian merchants at the beginning of the fourteenth century.

With the opening of more trade routes in the sixteenth and seventeenth centuries, large numbers of Oriental rugs were imported, and they were greatly prized by those Europeans who could afford them. However, it wasn't until well into the eighteenth century that these rugs were actually placed on floors—before this, they were used as hangings or as table covers. By the eighteenth century, carpetmaking itself had been transported to Europe, and French Savonnerie designs were soon to have an influence of their own on their Eastern forebears.

While Europeans were just discovering the Oriental rug, the Persians were creating their crowning masterpieces. In the sixteenth century, rugmaking reached its peak with the Safavid dynasty, whose dominions stretched far beyond the borders of present-day Iran. The capital of the Persian empire was the city of Isfahan, and the rugs, miniatures, and other treasures produced there for the court were the finest examples of the country's arts. The Safavid rugs were particularly beautiful, and with good reason. Well-known artists from all over the empire were brought to Isfahan to supervise their design, and the carpets themselves were finely worked in silk, with accents of gold and silver thread. With the decline of the Safavid dynasty in the eighteenth century, the production of the magnificent court rugs ceased. But the designs themselves endured and became the classic models for generations of weavers.

In the nineteenth century, as European demand for Oriental rugs rose, the West began to have an impact on the weaving centers of the East. Factories and workshops, which had originally been established to satisfy local needs, were expanded to meet the demands of foreign trade. The workers were closely supervised to assure the quality of their rugs, and the range of sizes they produced was expanded to include those that were better suited to European rooms.

These factories and workshops profited from the organization and innovation that had been brought to weaving by the craftsmen of the Safavid court. They employed highly skilled artisans who were able to produce intricate and sophisticated designs, and they also took advantage of advances in the technology of rugmaking that had occurred through the centuries. The preparation of the raw materials had improved, and the range of materials had also been expanded to include cotton, which provided a stronger foundation than wool. Loom construction had also been improved by the addition of mechanisms that enabled alternate threads to be separated so the weaving could proceed more smoothly.

What Is an Oriental Rug?

The patterns used in Oriental rugs had also come a long way. The early nomadic designs had evolved over the centuries from simple stripes of color to geometrical patterns, and finally to the more sophisticated curving shapes of the Safavids. All these designs were inspired by flowers, fruit, trees, animals, birds, clouds, the sun and moon, and even utilitarian objects such as vases and lamps. Architectural shapes, particularly those seen in Muslim mosques, were also common. In some rugs, these forms were simplified or stylized into abstract shapes, while in others they were reproduced in faithful detail. As time went on, each area developed its own style—its own repertoire of colors, weaves, and patterns—and assumed its own identity.

As more and more carpets were exported, the rug industry in the traditional weaving areas was revived by the large Western market. Naturally, the needs of foreign buyers became a dominant influence on carpet production in the Near East—and to ensure that the demand for good-quality, functional carpets would be met, European and American businessmen became deeply involved in the rug trade and began their own efforts to organize the local craftsmen. By the end of the nineteenth century, their influence had produced changes not only in the traditional colors, but also in designs and sizes.

Before World War II, American entrepreneurs had the upper hand, and many important weaving centers produced rugs that reflected the tastes of the American market. However, after the war many Americans turned to broadloom and the new wall-to-wall carpeting, while buyers on the Continent continued to prefer Orientals. This, coupled with the booming post-war European economy, meant that these countries, particularly Germany, increasingly dictated the styles and sizes of Oriental rugs produced for export.

European and American involvement in the rug trade also led, quite naturally, to Western study of the history and craft of weaving and to Western recognition of Oriental rugs as collectors' items and art objects. Turkish carpets had always been admired in Europe and America, but it wasn't until the late nineteenth century that Persian rugs were given the recognition they deserved. Today, magnificent pieces from all the traditional rug-producing countries are on display in museums and galleries throughout the United States and Europe, and fine Oriental rugs are eagerly sought after by Western collectors.

THE RUG INDUSTRY TODAY

As is the case in all the decorative arts, the development of weaving in the traditional rug-producing nations was profoundly affected by the cultural heritage and artistic traditions of each country, as well as by the historical currents that influenced each area's social and political structure—particularly the foreign influences that were introduced through conquest and migration. And in the twentieth century, the effects of international politics, economics, and social upheavals on the lifestyle of a country naturally include an effect on its rug industry.

Weaving is a tedious and financially unrewarding occupation, and in some countries it's given way as industrialization takes hold and social reforms are enacted. On the other hand, the rug-weaving industry can be an economic boon to relatively poor countries with large populations that represent a ready source of cheap labor. Weaving has also been established on an organized basis in a number of socialist countries, and in many other nations the government has sponsored rug-weaving as a cottage industry in order to provide additional income to farmers and agricultural workers.

Designs that have stood the test of time are now being woven in many countries, some of them quite distant from the areas in which they were originally developed and which gave them their names. Enterprising manufacturers are reproducing styles that were first popularized in the sixteenth century, as well as styles that were familiar to our nineteenth-century ancestors, but with subtle modifications in keeping with twentieth-century tastes.

The weaving industry in the major, nontraditional rug-producing countries such as India, Pakistan, and Romania has become particularly flexible in meeting the tastes of their foreign customers, and an impressive variety of colors, designs, and sizes is now being produced. Today you can choose from a larger array of rugs—from both traditional and nontraditional rug-producing countries—than has ever been available before. In fact, when it comes to Oriental rugs, it's now true that there's something for everyone.

CHAPTER II

How Oriental Rugs Are Made

 THE BASIC PRINCIPLES OF RUGMAKING ARE the same throughout the world, with a few variations that are common to certain areas. You may be surprised to learn that the weaving of a geometrically designed American Indian rug—sometimes called a Navajo blanket—uses practically the same technique as the elegant French Aubusson carpet with its intricate, curving pattern, or that the Moroccan pile rug is made in the same way as the Chinese.

Briefly, the process goes like this. Once the design is decided upon and a suitable loom is set up, a vertical foundation of threads (called warps) is laid. On this, rows of horizontal threads (called wefts) will be applied. The design can be formed by simply passing the wefts from side to side through the vertical foundation, forming a simple fabric, or by adding rows of knots in between the horizontal threads, and in the process hiding them from sight. When the weaving has been completed, the rug is taken off the loom and a number of finishing processes—such as shearing and cleaning—take place.

It's important to be familiar with the steps involved in this relatively unsophisticated process, not because you'll actually weave rugs yourself (although there certainly are worse things you could do with your time), but because a basic knowledge of the simple technique involved in a rug's construction will give you a better understanding of a final product that may seem very complex. In other words, the more you know about the craft of weaving, the greater self-confidence you'll have when it comes time to buy your rug.

THE DESIGN

The first step in the creation of any Oriental rug is its inspiration or goal—in other words, its design. The basic design of the rug will dictate how large a loom is needed, what materials will be used, and in what colors. Only after these decisions have been made will the actual weaving begin.

Nomadic rugs are usually woven by women, many of whom have been trained in the craft since they were children. These

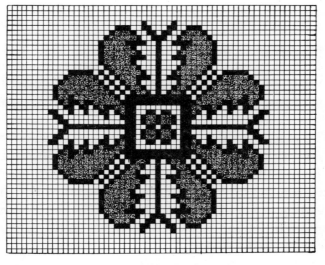

CARTOON

weavers have usually memorized a number of traditional patterns, and their choice of a design is limited to one of these. Occasionally, a nomad weaver will sketch a rough outline of a design on the vertical threads of her loom to serve as a guide, but it's just as com-

29

mon for her to improvise variations on a basic traditional pattern as she goes along.

On the other hand, village weavers, as well as those in the commercial workshops and factories, are usually guided by a detailed drawing of a specific design. This drawing, which is called a cartoon, is set down on graph paper; each square on the paper represents a single knot. Sometimes in the larger factories a number of identical rugs are produced at the same time. In this case, instead of giving each weaver a cartoon, a weaving master will recite the sequence of knots, and the weavers will follow this lead, tying knots in various colors as they're called out. Even if more than one weaver is at work on the same rug they can still both follow the weaving master because the design of the rug is almost always symmetrical—one half is the mirror image of the other.

THE LOOM

The basic design of the loom can be traced back to man's earliest days. In its simplest form, the loom is nothing more than a frame that's used to provide support for vertically placed threads (warps), upon which horizontal threads (wefts) are passed and knots are secured.

The most primitive weaving device, often referred to as a horizontal, or nomad, loom, is still in use today. It consists of two poles lying parallel on the ground, wrapped with warp threads that are held taut by stakes. The weaver begins work on this loom by squatting or kneeling in front of it, and as she progresses from the bottom to the top of the loom she sits on the part of the rug she's just finished weaving.

Simple horizontal looms are primarily used by itinerant tribesmen because they can be broken down and rolled up at a moment's notice. However, the fact that the nomad loom is so portable imposes certain limitations—nomad rugs are usually much smaller and narrower than rugs made on other types of looms.

Although nomad weaving is usually done by women, the

weaving in villages and towns—and in the rug factories—is done by both men and women. The simplest village weaving is a cottage industry, and as such it's done either in traditional patterns and colors or in variations dictated by entrepreneurs who supply materials for rugs that are woven to their own specifications.

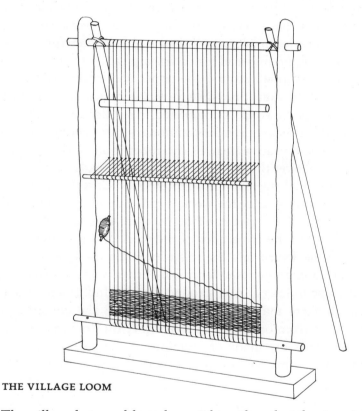

THE VILLAGE LOOM

The village loom, although upright rather than horizontal, is almost as primitive as the nomad loom. The weaver sits in front of this loom on a bench or a plank, and as the weaving progresses from the bottom to the top, the bench is raised higher and higher to keep level with the work—the weaver can end up perched several feet off the ground. As is true with the nomad loom, the rugs made on the village loom can be no longer than the distance between the upper and lower beams.

The Tabriz loom was developed for the urban rug factories

and workshops, and it's a sophisticated version of the village loom. However, unlike the village loom, the completed work on the Tabriz loom can be shifted to the rear by relieving the tension in the warp threads. This enables the weaver to sit at the same level throughout the entire weaving of the rug. Because of this shifting device, a rug woven on a Tabriz loom can be almost twice as long as the space between the upper and lower beams.

The roller loom takes the Tabriz loom one step further. It uses a separate supply of thread for each warp rather than a continuous warp that's wrapped around the upper and lower beams—an innovation that makes it possible to weave rugs in a greater variety of lengths. As the work is completed, it's rolled around the lower beam, and the weaver remains stationary throughout the weaving process. Another advantage of the roller loom is that it provides more control over the tension of the warp threads, and this means that the finished rugs have straighter sides. Unfortunately, there's also a drawback—since the work is rolled up as it's completed, the finished part of the rug can't be used as a design reference and compared with the remainder of the piece as it's woven.

Both the Tabriz and the roller loom are used in today's commerical weaving; the roller loom is a particularly important part of the cottage-industry rug production of India and Pakistan. Although there may be slight variations in the construction of these looms from one country to another (in Romania, for example, the looms are made of aluminum), the general structure of commercial looms remains the same throughout the world.

SETTING THE FOUNDATION

The first step in the weaving of a rug is to set up the threads of the vertical foundation (the warps) from the top of the loom to the bottom. The width of the finished rug will be the distance between the first and the last warp threads placed on the loom. Except for the case of the commercial roller loom, the warps aren't actually separate threads; instead they are formed by wrapping one

(Text continued on page 65)

PLATE I. *Tabriz*. Iran. 6′ x 4′4″.

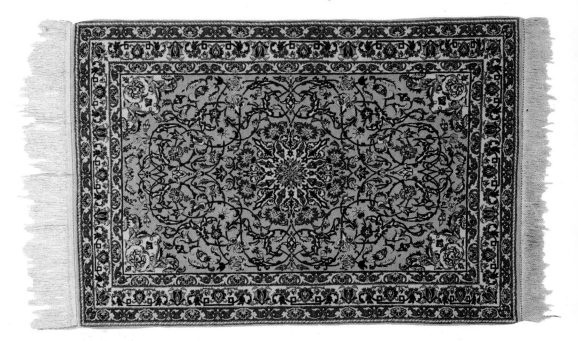

PLATE II. *Nain*. Iran. 3'7" x 2'7".

PLATE III. *Isfahan*. Iran. 7'7" x 5'.

PLATE IV. *Jozan Sarouk*. Iran. 7'3" x 4'3".

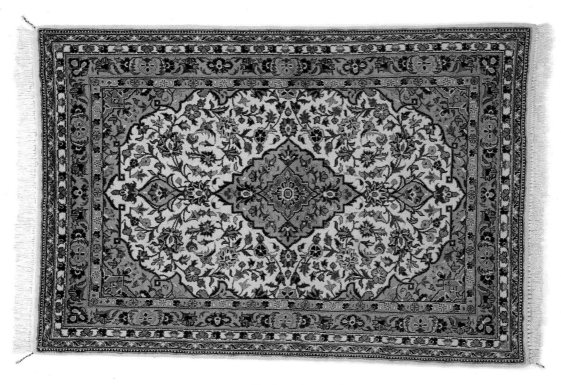

PLATE V. *Kashan*. Iran. 5' x 3'6".

PLATE VI. *Abadeh*. Iran. 5' x 3'6".

PLATE VII. *Joshagan*. Iran. 5' x 3'6".

PLATE VIII. *Karaje*. Iran. 6′4″ x 4′10″.

PLATE IX. *Afshar*. Iran. 6′10″ x 5′2″.

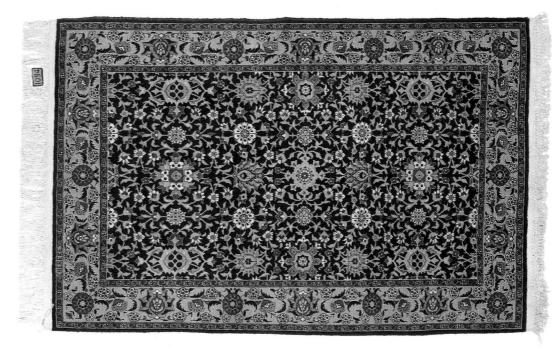

PLATE X. *Hereke*. Turkey. 5' x 3'5".

PLATE XI. *Kayseri*. Turkey. 7'6" x 5'.

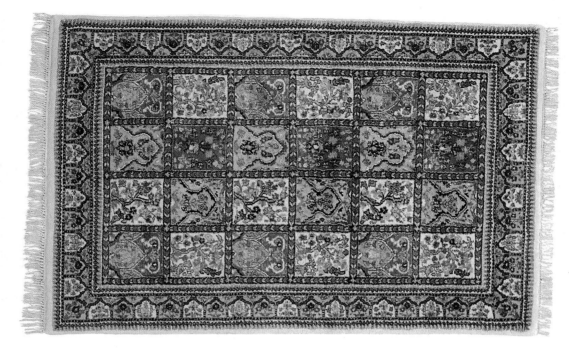

PLATE XII. *Indo-Tabriz*. India. 6' x 4'.

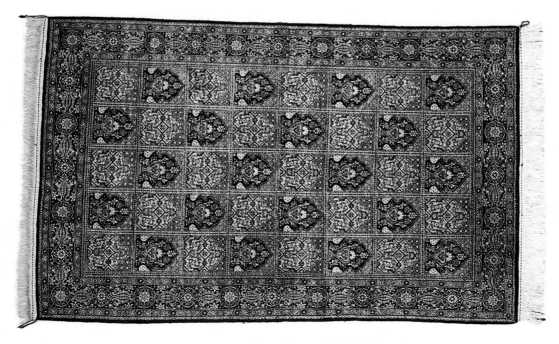

PLATE XIII. *Qum*. Iran. 5'5" x 3'6".

PLATE XIV. *Bidjar*. Iran. 5'4" x 3'4".

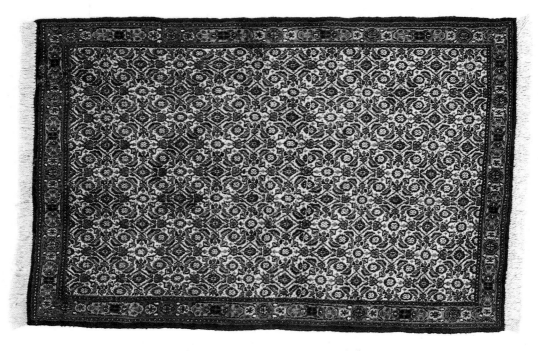

PLATE XV. *Mud*. Iran. 5' x 3'4".

PLATE XVI.   *Yalameh*. Iran. 5′ x 3′6″.

PLATE XVII.   *Shiraz*. Iran. 5′6″ x 3′6″.

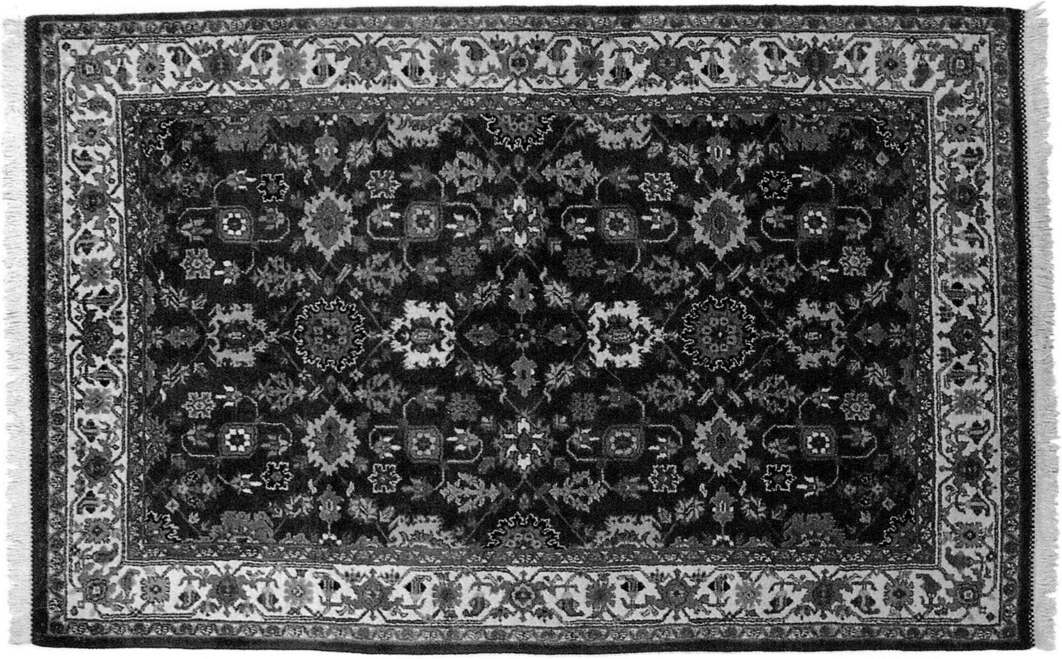

PLATE XVIII. *Indo-Minahani*. India. 9′ x 6′.

PLATE XIX. *Spanish*. Spain. 9′ x 6′.

PLATE XX. *Indo-Kashan*. India. 9′ x 6′.

PLATE XXI. *Injelas*. Iran. 4'10" x 3'5".

PLATE XXII. *Dergezine*. Iran. 4'5" x 2'10".

PLATE XXIII. *Sarouk*. Iran. 6′8″ x 4′2″.

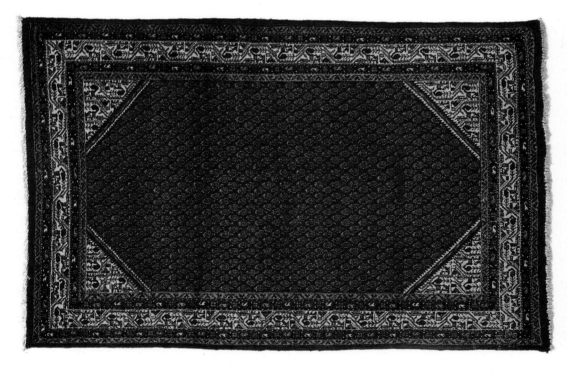

PLATE XXIV. *Mir-Sarouk*. Iran. 6′8″ x 4′5″.

PLATE XXV. *Indo-Qum*. India. 6′9″ x 4′2″.

PLATE XXVI. *Kashmir*. Pakistan. 7′2″ x 4′9″.

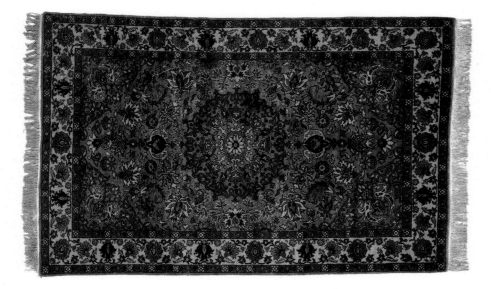

PLATE XXVII. *Bucharesti*. Romania. 6′5″ x 4′2″.

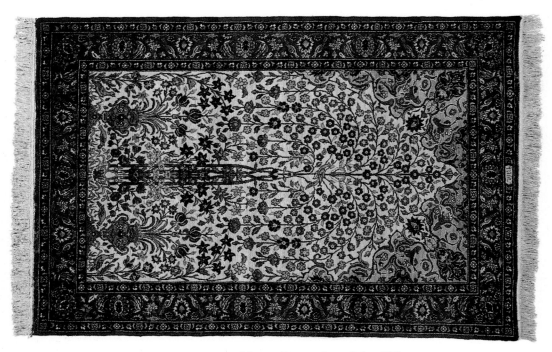

PLATE XXVIII. *Mures*. Romania. 6′3″ x 4′3″.

PLATE XXIX.　　*Ardebil.* Iran.　6'1" x 4'5".

PLATE XXX.　　*Meshkin.* Iran.　9'5" x 5'8".

PLATE XXXI. *Shiraz Kilim*. Iran. 8'10" x 4'10".

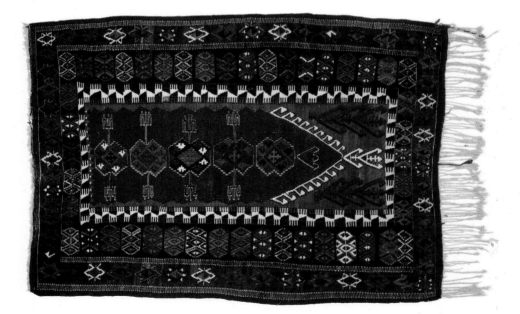

PLATE XXXII. *Kilim*. Turkey. 6'4" x 4'7".

PLATE XXXIII. *Herez*. Iran. 8′10″ x 6′1″.

PLATE XXXIV. *Bakhtiari*. Iran. 6′7″ x 4′4″.

PLATE XXXV.   *Saph*. Pakistan. 6'10" x 3'1".

PLATE XXXVI.   *Serab*. Iran. 7'3" x 3'2".

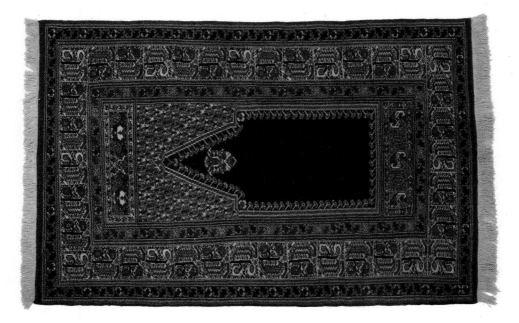

PLATE XXXVII.   *Kula*. Turkey. 6'10" x 4'8".

PLATE XXXVIII.   *Yaçebedir*. Turkey. 6' x 4'.

PLATE XXXIX. *Ladik*. Turkey. 6'2" x 4'3".

PLATE XL. *Milâs*. Turkey. 7' x 4'1".

PLATE XLI. *Chinese Aubusson*. China. 9′ x 6′.

PLATE XLII. *Kerman*. Iran. 6′ x 4′.

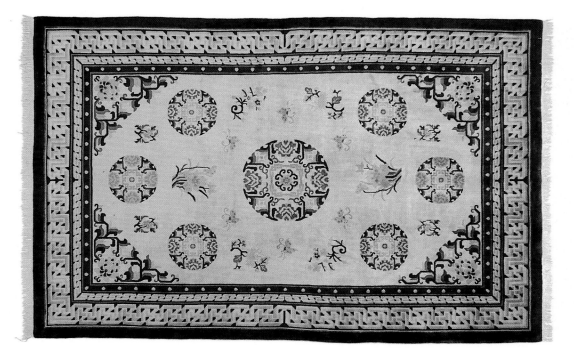

PLATE XLIII. *Chinese Antique Wash*. China. 9'1" x 5'10".

PLATE XLIV. *Chinese Goat Hair*. China. 6' x 4'.

PLATE XLV. *Indo-Aubusson*. India. 9′ x 6′.

PLATE XLVI. *Tai-Ming*. Taiwan. 6′ x 4′.

PLATE XLVII. *Chinese Silk*. China. 5′ x 3′.

PLATE XLVIII. *Peking*. China. 9′ x 6′.

PLATE XLIX.   *Bokhara*. Pakistan.   7'5" x 4'4".

PLATE L. *Afghan*. Afghanistan. 5' x 3'6".

PLATE LI. *Bokhara*. Iran. 4' x 3'.

PLATE LII. *Indo-Shirvan*. India. 6′2″ x 4′1″.

PLATE LIII. *Shirvan*. Pakistan. 5′9″ x 4′.

PLATE LIV. *Transylvanian*. Romania. 6'2" x 4'9".

PLATE LV. *Kazak*. U.S.S.R. 6' x 4'1".

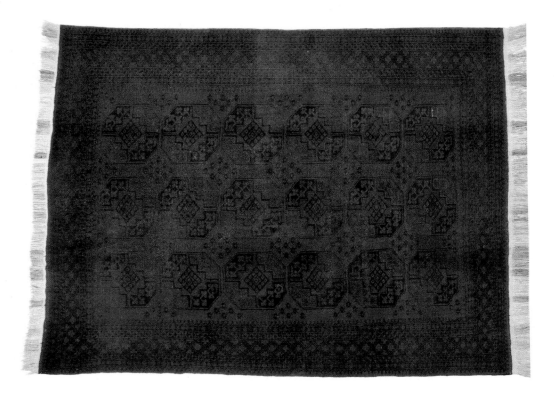

PLATE LVI. *Afghan*. Afghanistan. 10' x 8'.

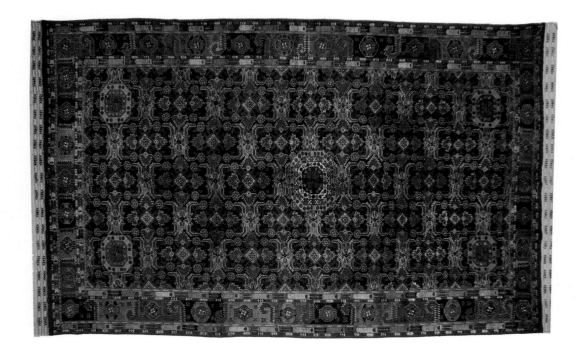

PLATE LVII. *Beshir*. U.S.S.R. 11'9" x 7'4".

PLATE LVIII.   *Belouch*. Iran. 6'4" x 3'10".

PLATE LIX.   *Belouch*. Afghanistan. 5'8" x 3'.

PLATE LX. *Chinese Dragon*. China. 8' x 5'.

continuous thread tightly around the upper and lower beams of the loom.

After the warps have been set up on the loom, the actual weaving begins. First, a horizontal (weft) thread is passed through alternate warp threads along the width of the loom. In all but the most primitive looms, this is done with the aid of a beamlike device called the heddle, which is attached to every other warp thread. Pulling on the heddle allows the warp threads to be separated, forming a tent-shaped hollow called the shed. The alternate set of warp threads can be moved by pulling another beam

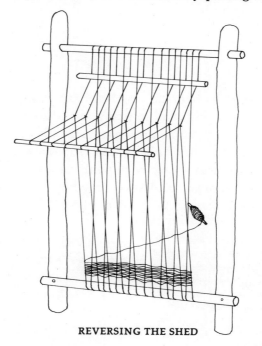

REVERSING THE SHED

called the lease rod. This moves the rear set of warp threads to the front, a process that's called, naturally enough, reversing the shed.

The shed must be reversed for a very simple reason. After a weft thread has been run across the width of the loom, it must go back in the other direction, but on the return journey it must pass in front of the other set of threads in order to be locked into place. To do this, the shed is reversed after each row of wefts has been inserted, a process that continues throughout the weaving of the rug. Another point to keep in mind is the fact that the warps tend to line up in front of or in back of each other whenever the shed is formed. This is called stacking the warps, and it means that when you look at the back of the rug the loops of each knot will also be stacked to some degree.

In pile rugs, the flat fabric that's produced by the meshing of the warps and wefts is only worked for a short distance, to provide a sturdy foundation before the knotting is begun. In other pieces, the flat weaving of the warps and wefts forms the finished fabric and no knots are added.

FLAT WEAVING

Flat-woven textiles were made long before there were pile carpets, and they're still woven today in many of the areas that also produce pile rugs. In fact, some areas produce only flat-woven rugs. The most common form of pileless rug is made with the tapestry technique. In this method, we begin with a loom and the familiar vertical foundation of warps. However, when the horizontal wefts are inserted, instead of serving merely to hold the pile in place,

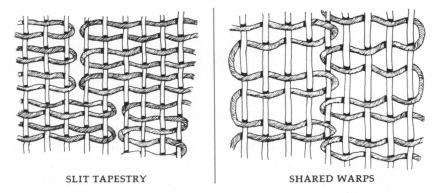

SLIT TAPESTRY   SHARED WARPS

they actually form the face of the carpet. The wefts are passed through alternating warps and are so tightly compressed that they hide the warp threads.

In the tapestry technique, patterns are formed by discontinuing one colored thread part way across the width of the rug, burying the loose end in the portion that's already been worked, and taking up the weaving again on the next warp with a different color. For this reason, it's not practical to use designs that incorporate vertical columns of the same color because this will create slits in the rug where the columns end. However, a number of techniques have been developed to overcome this problem. One is to incorporate crenellated rather than straight columns into the design. Another is to have adjacent colors share the same final warp threads, a method that's used by American Indian weavers. Two other solutions are to insert periodically a fine weft that's not part of the design, or to actually stitch any slits closed by hand. Kilims, dhurries, tapestries, and druggets—all flat-woven rugs—use one of these techniques.

You may also find flat-woven carpets done in the Soumak stitch. In this style of weaving, a weft is usually drawn over either two or four warps, then back under half of them, and so on and so forth, across and back. This produces a kind of herringbone effect on the face of the carpet, as well as a series of ridges on the back. Soumak carpets also have a single hidden weft inserted after every second row.

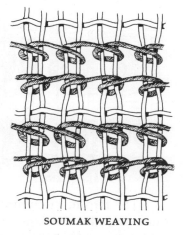

SOUMAK WEAVING

Obviously, all these flat-woven rugs are simpler to produce than pile rugs. They take less time to weave, and they tend to be less expensive. Since they're thinner than pile carpets they also tend to be less durable. Nevertheless, finely woven flat rugs can be sturdy, strikingly attractive, and versatile. They can be used on floors (as long as they're woven firmly enough to be stationary), on walls, and on furniture. Most are reversible, and all are easy to store.

KNOTTING

The knots in an Oriental rug are made by winding lengths of colored yarn around adjacent warps on the loom and then cutting off the ends of the yarn. The balls of colored yarn that the weaver uses to tie the knots are usually hung from the upper beam of the loom, within easy reach. Not a second is wasted as the weaver's fingers move from one set of warps to the next. It's not uncommon for an average skilled weaver to tie up to a thousand knots in an hour. In a workshop, each weaver covers about three to four feet of the width of a carpet, working as a team with several other weavers. If each of these weavers ties an average of ten thousand knots a day, they will still only finish an inch or two of a finely woven carpet. It can take a month or more for them to finish the entire piece.

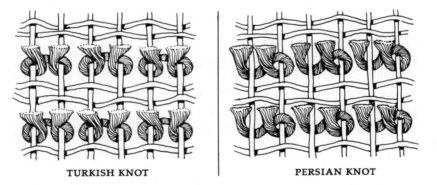

TURKISH KNOT   PERSIAN KNOT

The two most common knots are the Turkish, or Ghiordes, knot and the Persian, or Senneh, knot. The Turkish knot is primarily used in Turkey and the Caucasus, while the Persian knot is used further east, in India, Pakistan, and China. Iranian rugs can be woven in either Turkish or Persian knots, depending on the region or on the tribal tradition of the weaver. (For example, in Azerbaijan, the weavers use a device that's very similar to a crochet hook; this technique, which isn't found anywhere else in the world, can only be used to make Turkish knots.) However, Turkish and Persian knots are rarely used together in the same carpet; as a rule, every knot in a rug is tied in the same way.

In the Turkish knot, the ends of the yarn are brought forward together between two adjacent warps. However, in the Persian knot the yarn encircles the two warp threads, passing under one and around the other. In the Persian knot, the ends can face either to the left or to the right. This is why the Persian knot is also called the asymmetrical knot, as opposed to the symmetrical Turkish knot. Some experts have argued that a rug woven with Persian knots has a finer pile because all the warps are separated, but there's really very little practical difference between the two types of knots.

As the knots are made, the ends are roughly cut with a knife and the loops that are formed around the warps are pulled down toward the weaver and positioned above the loops in the previous row. Each knot is tied on the same warps as the knot directly below it. The cut ends of this mass of knots create the pile, which has a definite direction, or nap, that you can see by brushing your hand back and forth against the surface of the carpet.

There's no difference in the appearance of the pile of rugs that have been woven with the Turkish knot and the Persian knot—no matter which one is used, two strands of fiber are left showing on the face of the rug. However, with a very sharp eye you can often tell which kind of knot has been used by looking at the back of the rug. You'll remember from our description of setting the foundation that most rugs are woven with adjacent warp threads at different levels. When a Persian knot is tied on these warps, one loop of the knot lines up directly under the other, so only one loop or bump will be visible on the back of the rug. In other words, the Persian knot is stacked, by virtue of the way that it's tied. (As usual, there's always an exception to the rule—you'll find that in Turkoman carpets, and copies of Turkoman weavings, the Persian knot isn't stacked.)

With the Turkish knot, two loops or bumps will be visible. These loops may be on the same level, at any intermediate level, or even one on top of the other, as they are in the Persian knot. In the latter case, the position of the loops is dictated by stacking the warps on which the knots are tied.

It stands to reason that a rug that has finer warps will have more knots. After all, only as many knots can be placed in a row as there are pairs of warps to accept them. An easy way to gauge the fineness of the knotting in a particular rug is to look at the diameter of the warp threads that form the fringes at the ends. The only time this trick doesn't work is when the fringes aren't the original ones, or when an unscrupulous weaver has tied his knots over more than the standard two warps. This is called jufti, or false knotting, and it's never used by reputable weavers and manufacturers. Nevertheless, the jufti knot is sometimes found in the open, solid-colored field of apparently finely woven rugs, usually from Iran or Pakistan. (An easy way to detect jufti knotting is to compare the horizontal knot count to the number of warps in a particular area of the rug. If the number of knots is less than half the number of warps, you can be sure that jufti knots have been used.)

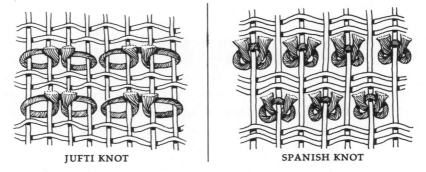

JUFTI KNOT   SPANISH KNOT

Another kind of knotting, which is much less common than the Persian or the Turkish—or the jufti—is a knot that's tied around a single warp. This method is used almost exclusively in Spanish carpets, and has been since the sixteenth century. The Spanish knot is tied on every other warp thread, and these are alternated with each row.

After the knots—Persian, Turkish, or whatever—have been tied in a row across the width of the rug, a weft thread is inserted and pushed or pounded down with a comb made of wood or iron. This secures the so-called knots—which, you'll recall, are laid around the warp threads rather than actually tied around them— and makes the pile part of the woven fabric of the carpet.

Actually, most rugs have at least two wefts (and sometimes

three or four) after every row of knots; the first weft is heavier and denser than the second, which is inserted after the shed has been reversed. When two wefts are used, each row of knots is tied with the threads at the same level and it's possible to hide any trace of the warps by compressing the pile. When a rug has only one weft, you'll be able to see a herringbone effect on the back—since the threads are woven on alternate levels at each row, a small portion of the warps will be left showing.

In addition to securing the knots, the weft threads have another important function. They give body to the rug because they aren't cut at the end of each row; but instead, they're simply passed back in the opposite direction. The wefts can either form the selvedge edges on the sides of the rug or be incorporated into them.

The setting of wefts and the tying of knots is the basic process that's repeated throughout the weaving of a pile carpet. First, a row of the pattern-forming knots is laid around the warp threads, then the weft threads are placed above them and pushed tightly against them, then the next row of knots is laid, and so on and on until the carpet reaches its intended length. At this point, another series of weft threads is inserted to make a flat, pileless edging, and the weaving is completed.

FINISHING

When the rug is removed from the loom, the loose warp ends are left as is or tied to form either a braided or a knotted fringe. Remember, this original fringe is actually part of the rug's foundation; the threads run through the entire length of the carpet. It's surprising how few people who own Oriental rugs are aware of this simple but important fact.

At the same time that the fringes are tied, the sides of the rug may be overcast, or a selvedge border may be added. On the other hand, this step may take place much later, after the rug has been exported.

Clipping

As the rug is being woven, the ends of each knot are roughly cut with a knife when the knot is inserted in the foundation. Sometimes another trimming takes place when each row of knots is completed or after several rows have been worked. After the whole rug is finished, it's carefully sheared once again to give it a uniform thickness. This final shearing is done either by laying the rug flat on the ground or by draping it over a beam. In the rug workshops and factories, a special worker is usually trained to perform this job. After all, an expert shearing finishes off the rug— but a botched shearing can ruin months of painstaking labor.

Certain rugs, particularly those from India and China, are also embossed or incised. In this process, a groove is cut partly through the pile where different colors meet. This creates a shadow when light shines on the carpet, accenting certain elements of the design. In finer rugs, these accents are produced by outlining designs with a single row of knots in a contrasting color. However, carpets that are embossed tend to be those with relatively simple designs, rugs that would have a flat appearance if they weren't given these variations in the depth of the pile.

Washing

After the rug is clipped, it's washed to remove any dirt that may have collected during the weaving and to give the finished rug its luster. In a great many areas, certain chemicals are added to the water when the rug is cleaned. This chemical wash, which is also called a reduction bath, removes short, staple pile fibers that absorb light. It also softens the tones of the colors in the rug.

Even though today's dyes are colorfast synthetics, they can be harsh and raw without chemical washing, which approximates shades that were once gained only by years of use. Chemical washing may occur in the country where the rug is made or at a regional collection center. It's also often done after the rugs have arrived in America.

Chemical washing is now practically universal. Although many years ago this kind of process may have been damaging to some kinds of rugs, today it's quite safe and effective. The older chemical washing was used to make rugs very shiny, but the modern process is intended only to mute the colors. For this reason, it's much less severe.

Another kind of chemical process, known as "gold washing," is sometimes used to bleach red tones out of certain carpets. Gold washing can occasionally weaken the pile fibers, but on the other hand, it can also give a rug quite a pleasing effect. However, there's one obvious drawback. If the bleach hasn't penetrated far enough, the dark colors will come to the surface as the rug wears. That's why you should always break open the pile yarn and look at the colors at the foundation when you're considering this kind of rug.

MATERIALS

Since the construction of a rug begins with the warps, it's natural to expect that this part of the foundation be made with a sturdy fiber. Today, most warps are made of cotton because it's strong and can be finely spun. It's also been found that wool seems to adhere to cotton, so the wool pile and the cotton foundation form a tight bond. Finally, cotton is dimensionally stable—this means that cotton, unlike wool, shrinks evenly when it's washed and stays flatter after it's dry.

Many older rugs have wool warps, and so do some of those that are made by nomadic tribes or by their sedentary descendants. Obviously, the choice of certain materials is influenced by local traditions and lifestyles. For example, nomadic weavers obviously have no opportunity to spin their own cotton. On the other hand, commercial rug factories have a much wider selection of materials. In addition to cotton, silk or linen warps are sometimes used in these centers for the weaving of extremely fine rugs.

Like the warps, the wefts used in today's carpets are generally made of cotton. However, rugs that have wool warps usually also have wool wefts. Silk is used for wefting only in rugs that have silk pile. As for the pile, the chances are that the carpet you buy today will be knotted in wool. However, animal hair, particularly camel and goat hair, is also used. In addition, silk is sometimes used as an accent in wool-pile rugs, and in the case of very fine rugs it's the only fiber used for the knotting.

For the most part, though, the vast majority of Oriental rugs are knotted in wool. This wool may not necessarily come from the same area in which the carpet was made. Today, as has been the practice for decades, if native wool isn't available or isn't suitable, it's blended with imported wool. This is especially true of the wool used in the workshops and factories.

Wool can vary a good deal in quality, depending on the climate of the region in which the sheep were raised, the part of the sheep the wool came from, the season in which the shearing took place, and even the age of the animal. It's also important that the wool be taken from live sheep, since the wool from dead animals is brittle and dull.

Sometimes the sheep is washed before it's shorn, but usually the wool is washed after the shearing. Then the wool is carded (a teasing process that lengthens and straightens the fibers) and spun, either by machine or by hand. Finally, the threads of the spun wool are twisted together (in the opposite direction from which they were spun) to form the yarn itself. Each thread that goes into the yarn is called a ply, and the more plies the yarn has the thicker and stronger it is.

Once the yarn has been through all these preliminary steps it's ready to be dyed. The subject of dyes used to be quite a lively one, filled with arcane descriptions of tribal formulas and debates over the superiority of this or that natural or vegetable dye. While this can be fascinating, the fact is that there's very little left to argue about. Obviously, the quality and depth of color supplied by dyes play a crucial part in the design of any rug, but the composition of the dyes themselves no longer varies from one region to another. Today, the vast majority of rugs from all the major production centers are woven with chrome-dyed wool. Only a few rugs from remote villages in Iran, Turkey, and Afghanistan are still made with wool dyed with vegetable or natural dyestuffs.

It's important not to confuse chrome dyes with aniline dyes, which were first discovered in the mid-nineteenth century. These early products were very crude and produced harsh colors. In addition, over the years it became apparent that they could be damaging to wool. Around the turn of the century, aniline dyes were banned in Iran and a number of other countries, and their use was quite controversial well into the twentieth century. However, great advances were made in chemical dyes between the two World Wars, and today's dyestuffs bear little resemblance to their predecessors. Unfortunately, the bad reputation of the early aniline dyes has lingered on, and often leads to unfair criticism of today's much more reliable chrome dyes.

Aside from the advantages afforded by their uniformity and the fact that they're relatively inexpensive, chrome dyes are also preferred by manufacturers because they can be produced in a wide range of colors, including almost all the shades that were once available using natural dyestuffs. It's ironic that these modern dyes have been criticized because of their comparative permanence and that so-called vegetable dyes are revered because they fade more easily—even though that fading doesn't always produce a pleasing color. In addition, while some purists are quick to remind us of how much damage the old aniline dyes caused, they seem to forget that certain natural dyes have also been known to have harmful effects. Again, this isn't the case with chrome dyes. Modern dyes also eliminate the condition known as "abrash," the occasionally unpleasant variation in color that's usually found in nomad rugs.

The important thing to remember about dyes is that color fastness is the ultimate test of an effective dye. Any fabric that's placed in direct sunlight will fade, no matter what it's been dyed with. But a rug in which chrome dyes have been used will fade more evenly, and its colors will remain fast—that is, one color won't bleed into another. Rest assured, then, that chrome dyes are perfectly reliable. As a rug buyer, your only concern should be the colors themselves and the combinations in which they're used, not the composition of the dyes that produced them.

CHAPTER III

WHERE TO BUY
AN ORIENTAL RUG

 ONE OF THE MOST IMPORTANT FACTORS TO consider when you're buying an Oriental rug is *where* you buy that rug. With so many rugs to choose from, in so many styles and qualities, it's crucial that you have confidence in the knowledge and reliability of the person you're buying from. Working with a responsible expert is the safest way of buying a rug, the way that involves the least risk to you. That's why I recommend that you buy only from an established, reputable dealer, a dealer who maintains a showroom especially for the purpose of selling Oriental rugs.

I also recommend that you go about selecting your rug slowly and carefully. Don't rush out and buy a rug from the first dealer you visit. Go to a number of stores and ask yourself (and the dealers) a few questions along the way.

Look at the store itself. What kind of an image does it have? Is it neat, clean, well lighted, and well organized? Does it seem to have a sufficient stock of merchandise from a variety of sources and in a range of sizes? Remember that a large inventory represents a significant investment on the part of the dealer; he's committed a lot of money to his business, and this means he has a commitment to making it work. On the other hand, a dealer who has just a few rugs has made no real investment in his business—he'll be tempted to give you a hard sell for the rugs he has instead of helping you find the one that's right for you.

Consider the personnel in the store. Are the people you meet knowledgeable, or are they constantly referring to the tags on the rugs before they tell you what kind they are? Are the sales people courteous and patient? Do they have any decorating skills? Do they try to sell you rugs that they like, or are they interested in pleasing your tastes? If they don't have exactly what you want will they offer to get it for you—without obliging you to buy the rug? Ask for their opinions on size and durability and pay close attention to the answers you're given.

Once you've visited a showroom, ask your friends and acquaintances about the store; see if it has an established clientele. Remember, though, that the length of time a company has been in business may tell you more about its reputation than its expertise. After all, a new shop may be owned and run by someone with years of experience working for another dealer. On the other hand, it *is* comforting to know that a particular dealer is established in the community and will be around if you have any unforeseen problems. An established dealer is also more apt to offer a variety of payment plans.

Above all, an established dealer is usually willing to let you try a rug at home before you commit yourself to buying it. By trying the rug at home, you'll be able to see how it looks under your own lighting conditions, both during the day and at night, and you can see whether the rug is compatible with your furniture and your decorating scheme. You'll also be able to take all the guesswork out of determining the right size. Most important, you'll be able to have enough time to examine the rug carefully, to live with it a little while and find out whether it really suits you.

It pays to be careful and deliberate when you're shopping for a rug. Visit a number of reputable dealers and keep track of what you see, what you like, and how much the various rugs cost. To get a rough idea of the size you'll need, sketch out the dimensions of your room (and the furniture in it) on the pages provided in the Appendix. Use the photographs in the color portfolio as a guide when you're considering different colors and designs, and take notes on what you see at various shops. (You'll find room for these notes in the Appendix too.)

While you're making your rounds, ask a lot of questions and see as many rugs as you can. Make careful comparisons and don't rush into anything. And remember that certain situations should be approached with caution.

SALES PRACTICES

Just about every merchant has a sale at one time or another, and naturally there are legitimate reasons for having them. Many rug dealers run sales promotions to add to their business and to raise money to buy more rugs. However, you must know something about the dealer—and why he's having a sale—before you buy from him.

Don't be overly impressed simply by the fact that there's a sale. Find out for yourself if in fact you're going to be saving any money; compare the sale prices with the regular prices at other stores. You may be surprised to find that there's very little difference between them. The fact is that some dealers seem to run sales almost continuously, while others start off with inflated presale prices. Above all, see if there's anything on sale that appeals to you. Don't buy a rug that you're not totally sure of simply because the price is so reasonable—never underestimate the cost of looking at and living with a rug that doesn't suit you or your decor.

Some dealers attempt to appeal to buyers by claiming that they feature direct importation of rugs, implying that some of the middleman's costs will be eliminated along the way. Many dealers do in fact import goods directly from the rug-producing countries, but it's also true that few dealers do so exclusively. Quite frankly, there's not so much to be gained by this. It's unlikely that any dealer can afford to have his own resident buying agent in every exporting country, and a dealer who travels periodically will find only what's available at that particular time. He'll also be faced with large shipping and handling expenses. In most cases, any savings that result from direct importation are usually small—and the sacrifices can be large.

Another thing to remember about direct importation is that it sometimes imposes limitations on the varieties and qualities of rugs that you'll be able to see in a particular shop. Most rug production is done under contract between a manufacturer and a wholesaler. This means that a dealer who's importing rugs directly has usually bought them in bazaars or other spot markets—but rugs from these sources aren't always of the best quality, and the selection is usually limited. In fact, many of the rugs in the bazaars are pieces that have been rejected by the wholesalers.

At this point, it may occur to you that the best way to get a bargain on an Oriental is to bypass a retailer and buy wholesale. But this tactic isn't usually very successful, mainly because most wholesalers specialize in certain kinds of rugs. True wholesalers usually aren't interested in competing with their dealers, and even if you find one who'll let you buy, the odds are that he won't extend you home trial or credit, or other privileges.

Occasionally you'll read advertisements claiming that the rugs in a particular shop have been woven especially for the dealer. This is probably an exaggeration. With perhaps one or two exceptions, no wholesalers or importers, let alone retailers, have exclusive weaving arrangements in any country. Besides, even if such a claim is true, it only means that you'll have a more difficult time judging the quality of a particular rug because you won't be able to compare it with similar rugs at other shops.

The fact that a dealer claims a liberal trade-in policy is also no special reason to buy from him. If the rug is well made and was originally sold at a fair price, you shouldn't have any problem trading it in against another purchase with *any* reliable dealer. So why limit your options?

Mail-order sales are another feature offered by some dealers, but they're a very limited way of buying rugs. You should consider buying by mail *only* if you're unable to visit a showroom to see finished rugs firsthand. Why? Because the only rugs you'll get to look at are those that will be sent to you. Shopping in a store is always preferable to shopping by mail, not only because it's educational, but also because it's far easier to communicate in person. You can see practically every rug a mail-order house has to offer—and many more—at a dealer's showroom, and you'll be spared the handling charges, freight costs, and other problems involved in receiving and returning rugs sent to you on approval.

If there are no rug dealers in your area, it would be more practical for you to telephone several dealers in nearby cities to see whether they have anything that meets your needs and then make the investment in a trip. That way, you'll be giving yourself the opportunity to choose from the widest selection of rugs available. You may even discover new possibilities that you might not have considered if you hadn't actually seen the rugs yourself.

Although it's reasonable to expect a dealer to have a wide variety of rugs, you should also realize that it's impossible for him to have everything in stock. Oriental rugs are available in countless combinations of colors, designs, and sizes. Many dealers try to solve this problem by offering a catalog from which you can choose rugs that aren't in the shop's current inventory. A well-produced catalog can give you a good idea of what a rug will look like, but you should never buy a rug solely on the basis of a photograph. Even the color photographs in this book, which are of very good quality, can't convey the exact look of the rugs themselves—after all, how can a two-dimensional reproduction show you everything there is to see in the three-dimensional original?

Catalog buying can be an acceptable way to buy a rug only if you can see a reasonably sized sample rug in the identical colors, design, and quality of the rug you're interested in buying. You should also be allowed to take the sample home. If there's no sample available, be certain that you're under no obligation to buy the rug of your choice without actually seeing it and perhaps even trying it at home.

Where To Buy An Oriental Rug

Auctions

One of the best ways a rug buyer can avoid making costly mistakes is simply to avoid any kind of auction. New rugs are rarely sold at old, established auction houses, and if they do appear, you can be sure that they've been consigned by a dealer. Almost all of these sales are conducted with a reserve—that is, the article won't be sold below a certain price that's been set by the consignor. And you can be sure that this reserve won't be less than the market value of the rug.

There's no legitimate reason for a dealer to sell his goods at auction unless the rugs are damaged or the dealer is in the business of conducting such sales, and in that case he'll certainly be sure to protect his merchandise. I've often heard buyers claim that since they were competing with a dealer at an auction their winning bid had to have been only a fraction over the wholesale value of the rug—in other words, that they'd saved a lot of money. However, contrary to the common belief, there's no honor in outbidding a dealer, for the rug you buy may be his own. Dealers simply don't buy new rugs at auction.

Aside from the fact that there are no bargains to be found among rugs put up for auction, there are still other disadvantages to this method of buying. Obviously, when you buy at auction you won't have the advantages of home trial, and, of course, you'll be seeing a very limited selection of rugs. You'll also be unable to return your rug if you decide you dislike it—or if you discover that it has some flaws. Many times, new rugs appearing at auctions have been damaged during shipment, have colors that run or irregular shapes, or are simply poorly made. Many of these problems may not be apparent without a careful inspection.

The short-notice auctions advertised in newspapers and normally held in a public room at a motel or hotel are even more hazardous for the novice than conventional auctions, and they're to be avoided at all costs. What they are, in essence, are high-pressure sales; they aren't really auctions at all. In fact, the rugs are often owned either by the auctioneer or by a single consignor, and you can be sure that they won't be sold at sacrifice prices. In addition, you'll usually be bidding against shills placed in the small audience by the auctioneer. The odds are that you'll end up paying more for a rug at one of these sales than you would if you had carefully shopped among a number of reliable dealers. Of greater importance, without the benefit of home trial you may quickly learn to dislike a rug that you bought on impulse.

Don't be fooled by any of the liberal trade-in policies claimed by the people running short-notice auctions. Read the presale advertisements *carefully*. They're almost always full of double-talk. I assure you that you'll be at the auctioneer's mercy (if you can find him) when you try to trade in a rug you bought at one of these sales. And even if you're successful you won't have much bargaining power—after all, you can only trade for what he has in his limited inventory.

Private Sales

Another situation you should approach with the utmost suspicion is an offering of rugs for sale by a private individual. In fact, you should *never* buy a new rug from a private seller. Such people may have little knowledge of rugs and they'll usually have a very small inventory; they certainly won't have any bargains. Occasionally, they may actually be dealers hiding behind the door of a house instead of operating out of a store, and you'd be wise to wonder just why they must resort to this practice.

Remember that an established dealer must meet certain obligations in order to stay in business. Dealers must invest in and maintain large, expensive inventories, and this means that there is an implied warranty that their rugs are fit for their intended use. Private offerings have none of these safeguards. You'll be buying with little or no choice as to color, quality, design, or size—and you'll have no recourse after you've made your purchase. You'll also have to pay the full price at the time you buy the rug.

When you buy from a private seller, the chances are that, rather than buying a rug, you'll be buying a story. To prove this, if you feel yourself yielding to temptation, ask the seller whether you can try the rug at home and tell him you're going to have it independently appraised. It's likely that he'll try to discourage you—and that should be the only danger signal you need.

FOREIGN BUYING

Buying a rug while you're traveling abroad can be just about as dangerous as buying at auction or buying from a private seller. You won't have reliable information about the dealer's reputation, and of course you won't be able to try the rug at home. Naturally, you'll simply be stuck with the rug if you get home and discover that the color, design, or size isn't right. In addition, you'll also be faced with the complexities of shipping, handling, and duties.

It's also likely that the rugs you buy abroad won't have been properly serviced. It's a rare rug indeed that doesn't need at least a minimum of further attention after it's "completed," and this is one of the many functions of a reputable dealer. We'll discuss this in more detail in Chapter V; for the time being, just resign yourself to finding a less expensive (and less risky) souvenir.

All these warnings and cautions may have convinced you that buying an Oriental rug can be a frustrating and perilous experience, but it need not be if you go about it the right way. All it really involves is remembering three simple rules: (1) Take your time and look around. (2) Buy only from a reputable dealer. (3) Buy only after you've tried your selection at home. And don't forget to exercise some common sense—be reasonable. Don't expect a single dealer to have everything in stock. Be conscious of the variety of colors, designs, and qualities that can be carried in any inventory, as well as the limitations that may be inherent in various types and styles of rugs. Be somewhat flexible when you're trying to determine what sizes, colors, and designs will meet your own particular needs. Don't concentrate on getting a bargain; instead, look at a range of prices, styles, and colors and find a rug that pleases you on every count. Above all, don't allow yourself to be pressured into buying—don't buy a story.

CHAPTER IV

COLOR, DESIGN, & SIZE

 WHEN YOU'RE SELECTING AN ORIENTAL RUG, your first thoughts turn to three basic considerations—color, design, and size. Since size is the most straightforward of the three, we'll save it for last. That leaves us with color and design. As far as I'm concerned, these are the two most important elements involved in buying a rug—that is, if you've followed my advice on *where* to buy a rug. To simplify things even further, you can say that color is the most important factor in choosing a rug. Color is to an Oriental rug as location is to real estate.

COLOR

Color is obviously a function of dyes. As we saw in Chapter II, up until the last century dyes were produced by local craftsmen from the animals and plants they found around them. Leaves, bark, berries, and even insects were used in secret formulas that were often handed down for generations within a single family, tribe, or village. Although these natural dyes could produce soft, deep colors that mellowed over the years, there were also some drawbacks involved in their use. In some areas, there was a very limited number of materials that could be used as dyestuffs, and naturally this meant that the range of colors would also be limited. In addition, the dyes themselves were sometimes poorly applied and at times they reacted poorly with minerals in the local water. This often resulted in the streaky unevenness of shade called "abrash," a defect that can be charming—but can just as easily be unsightly.

Other problems were caused when the raw wool was too dark, making it impossible to work with light colors. Some colors—particularly green, brown, black, and deep red—also proved difficult to dye because they had to be applied in such quantities that they could have a corrosive effect on the wool. Using large amounts of dye also created the risk of saturating the fibers, which might later bleed to adjoining areas worked in lighter colors.

Finally, once a scheme of colors had become acceptable, the local weavers were often reluctant to introduce any major changes. In fact, over the years some traditional color schemes, and the use or avoidance of certain colors, came to be surrounded by myths and superstitions. It's important to remember that most of these practices—such as the "sacred" taboo against using green because it's the color of the Prophet—really have their roots in the very practical consideration of whether or not a certain color is difficult to dye.

As we mentioned earlier, modern synthetic dyes are vast improvements over the crude aniline dyes that were first introduced in the mid-nineteenth century. In any event, for all practical purposes arguments about the virtues of vegetable, natural, synthetic, or chemical dyes are strictly academic. The fact is that you have little if any choice in the matter. Virtually all new Oriental rugs imported into the United States are made with chrome dyes. These dyes have proven their mettle and aren't destructive to wool, and you shouldn't have any hesitation about buying a rug in which they've been used. However, this doesn't mean that chrome dyes won't be produced in unpleasant shades and used in unsatisfactory combinations.

When you're looking at a new Oriental rug, you should make your color decision solely on the basis of whether or not what you see appeals to you. Remember that the new dyes are more stable than the old natural dyes. As the years pass, they won't mellow in the same way that natural dyes will. In other words, you should make your choice on the basis of the original color of the rug. The colors you see when you buy the rug will be more or less the permanent colors.

Once you've made basic decisions on your color preference, there's another factor to be considered. Despite the widespread use of modern chemical dyes, weavers in many areas continue to work with the same range of colors they've used in the past. It's still true that certain colors and combinations can be identified with certain geographical areas, and that the total palette of colors used in a particular region can be quite limited. For instance, you'll find that rugs produced by Turkoman and Afghan weavers are still done in predominantly red tones. The general descriptions of the rug-producing countries in Chapter VII and the directory of rug types in Chapter VIII will give you a clear idea of what colors are traditionally associated with particular areas. If you pay close attention to this information, you won't find yourself searching in vain for a combination of colors that doesn't exist or for certain colors that are never made in a certain design.

On the positive side, you should know that there's a greater variety of colors available today than there ever has been before. Today's market also offers a broader range of designs in a broader range of color combinations. For example, rugs made in the Kashan district of Iran are now available not only in the traditional ruby red or blue background, but also in ivory and cream (PLATE V), and the classic Shah Abbas pattern of Kashan is reproduced in India in an even wider range of light shades (PLATE XX). Classic red Turkoman designs (PLATE LVI) are woven in other countries in a variety of other colors (PLATE XLIX).

This greater range of colors and designs is available because of the increasing responsiveness of the rug-producing countries to the tastes of foreign markets as they recognize that the rug industry can be a viable source of revenue. However, despite this greater flexibility, you'll still find that compromises must sometimes be made. If you're faced with the dilemma of choosing between a color you like and a design you like, the color of the rug should be the most important consideration—for the simple reason that colors, unlike designs, don't seem to grow on you. Over the years, your color preferences will tend to stay the same; your design preferences may not.

Design

Theoretically, it's possible to produce an Oriental rug in which each and every knot is a different color. But, of course, it's far more interesting to produce knots in a pattern, and over the years certain basic design-forming combinations have evolved.

There are a number of different ways to talk about the "design" of Oriental rugs. First, there are certain general elements that make up the basic design of almost any rug—what you might call the different parts of a rug's design. Then there are a number of different basic types of design, as well as the particular patterns that are used in them. We'll discuss all of these in the pages that follow, not so much with the idea that you should memorize them, but simply so you can get a general idea of some of the possible combinations you'll run across, and which ones you like better than others.

The vast majority of Oriental rugs are made in the shape of a rectangle, and the two basic elements of this rectangular design are the field (or ground) and the borders. In most rugs, the field is the large central area of the design. One of the most common fields consists of one or more medallions, centered and standing alone (PLATE XLII). This is called, naturally enough, an open-field medallion design. A medallion, or a series of medallions, can also be used in a covered-field design, and in this case the medallion forms the central point from which the other smaller patterns flow (PLATES I, XI, XXXIII). The field might also be made up of a small repetitive pattern, with or without medallions or central figures (PLATE XV), or else it may be divided into several compartments (PLATE XXXIV).

In many Oriental rugs, the corners of the field also have

distinctive patterns. These are often quartered sections of the central medallion that have been positioned in each corner (PLATE V). However, in other rugs, the corner section may be quite different from the medallion (PLATE XI).

The border of an Oriental rug is usually made up of a main band, or stripe, surrounded by narrower bands, all forming a frame around the field of the rug. There can be quite a number of stripes in the border, or there can be only a few. There will, however, almost always be one main stripe. The narrower stripes that surround it are called secondary, or guard, stripes. And if a stripe is very narrow—only one or two knots wide—it's often called a line. Finally, some rugs may have a broken border—a pattern that extends into the field of the rug and is much more closely related to the field pattern than other borders are. These are usually seen in Oriental versions of French patterns.

You'll find the general design of a field surrounded by borders in almost all pile carpets. The only exceptions are some Chinese rugs, and Indian and Tibetan copies of Chinese rugs. In many cases, these designs consist only of large, randomly placed symbols, or an entire scene, without any borders.

Flat-woven rugs, or kilims, made with the tapestry technique may also depart from the traditional border and field arrangement. Sometimes a kilim's design will simply be a series of stripes running across the width of the rug. However, it's also common for a kilim to have the same basic design elements as a pile carpet (PLATE XXXI and XXXII).

The traditional design elements used in Oriental rugs were first inspired by familiar forms the weavers saw in the world around them. Animals, birds, insects, clouds, trees, mountains, lakes, and rivers were all reproduced in the weavers' patterns, and so were the objects and architectural shapes found in their homes and holy places. To these were added religious symbols, mythological creatures, and scenes from history and folklore. In other words, weavers of Oriental rugs have had the same kind of inspiration that's been common to artists since the earliest times. And, as in all the other arts, the medium itself imposed certain restrictions on how these inspirations were translated into designs.

You'll remember from Chapter II that practically every rug begins as a drawing on graph paper, with each square representing a single knot, very much as it does in a needlepoint pattern. These small, square knots are worked in different colors to form the design of the rug. The square shapes of the knots, the dimension and height of the pile, and the dimensions of the rug itself all have an effect on the look of the finished rug; they tend to obscure a design and flatten it out. This means that in some rugs only a few kinds of patterns will be successful. However, in other rugs these limitations can be overcome, through fine knotting and careful use of color, to create a feeling of depth and a sense of perspective—what's basically a geometrical arrangement of squares can be made to produce the illusion of perfectly curving shapes.

Obviously, the more knots there are in every square inch of a rug, the more intricate and curving its design can be. It's easy to see, then, why coarse rugs tend to be geometric and finer rugs tend to have more intricate and less angular designs. It's also easy to see why the diagram of the knots in a rug has often been compared to a musical score.

To carry the comparison one step further, the design of a rug, just like a musical score, incorporates repeats of its basic theme. In other words, there isn't actually a diagram for every single knot in a rug. Instead, the designs themselves are broken down into a square format that can be used either horizontally or vertically. This grid (or a combination of several grids) is repeated throughout the rug, making it possible to produce a pattern that twists and turns and appears in different directions without being distorted. This is possible because, with very rare exceptions, the basic design unit has virtually the same number of knots both horizontally and vertically.

Because their basic elements usually represent plants and animals, it's generally believed that the designs used in the fields of Oriental rugs were originally intended to bring the beauty of the outdoors inside. In many patterns, leaves, rosettes, blossoms, palmettes, and other floral figures are joined together by intertwining vines and arabesques. The same figures are often represented on geometric rugs, but sometimes so abstractly that they're unrecognizable. Naively drawn stick-like figures of humans and animals are also often seen in these geometric rugs— but in a finely woven piece they can be reproduced as realistically as in any painting.

The abstraction of many traditional designs can also be traced to the fact that one sect of Islam, the Sunnite, doesn't permit the depiction of living creatures. However, the Shiite sect, which is predominant in Iran, has never adhered to this belief, and Iranian carpets can be either realistic or elegantly stylized.

When we talk about the overall design, or style, of an Oriental rug we often use the name of the city, region, or tribal group with which that pattern has come to be associated. However, many of these patterns have been widely copied, and the traditional name itself is no longer a sure indication of where a rug was produced.

This trend didn't begin with the development of the modern rug industry in India, Pakistan, and the Far East. It's been going on for centuries, ever since rugs have been used as trading commodities. As soon as this process began, weavers came into contact with designs and techniques that were being used in other areas. Naturally, as they saw which designs were the most popular, they began to weave more and more rugs in these styles. Ever since rug weaving became an industry, it's been receptive to the demands of the consumer, and when you get right down to it, this means that almost all the "traditional" designs that are found in Oriental rugs have been influenced to some extent by the Western marketplace.

The most popular rug types—names like Shirvan, Shiraz, or Kashan—will be found in the directory in Chapter VIII. In this chapter, we'll stick to the basic elements that are used to form the designs of these different styles of rugs, and to certain general designs—such as the prayer rug—that are made in many different styles.

Color, Design, & Size

There are a great many classic design elements, and they're seen in rugs throughout the world. The two most commonly used in repeating patterns are the boteh (page 188), a figure that's usually described as a pear, a leaf, or a pine cone (and familiar to Westerners as the paisley pattern), and the Herati, or Feraghan, which consists of a rosette inside a diamond, which in turn is flanked by four curled leaves that can also sometimes resemble stylized fish (page 28). Another well-known element that's used in repeating designs is an octagonal lozenge shape known as a gul (page 84).

Other common design elements include the Minahani (page 180), in which large colorful rosettes are combined with diagonal vines to form an all-over pattern of diamonds superimposed on one another; the guli hinnai, in which rows of flowers and plants are surrounded by small floral sprays; and the Shah Abbas, the classic all-over pattern in which symmetrical intertwining vines are linked with palmettes (page 21). The Shah Abbas pattern often includes cloud bands, gently curving design elements borrowed from the Chinese and based, of course, on the shape of clouds (page 15). Other commonly used figures from the natural world include the tarantula, the crab (page 109), and the snake, as well as hundreds of stylized flowers. The latter are often worked in an all-over detached floral design, in which sprays of flowers are spread on a plain-colored field.

All these patterns have been used in rug-making countries throughout the world, and naturally the variations on the basic shapes are countless. In fact, even the Arabic calligraphy with which inscriptions and dates were woven into carpets has probably been the model for other graceful and curving stylized shapes.

The design elements used in the borders of rugs have also spread from one weaving district to another. In general, however, there's not as much variation in the borders as there may be in the field designs, simply because the options within such a restricted space are limited. You can't tell where a rug has been made just by looking at its borders. These designs can be similar in carpets that have been made within a rug-weaving district—and also in those from other countries.

The major stripe in the border often contains a repeating floral design. The most common is a form of meandering vine with imaginatively colored leaves, flowers, rosettes, or palmettes. This can be worked in both curving and geometric styles. Some border arrangements have become so well known that they've acquired labels, such as the turtle (page 144), the key, and the scroll; or the wine cup and the serrated leaf (page 115). The border often includes a number of guard stripes, and these may repeat the main border design or be made up of simpler geometric shapes. Almost all these border designs encircle the rug—in other words, they're repeated on all four sides.

Most of the classic border and field designs are used throughout the world, but there's one area that departs from this practice. Although some common elements—such as cloud bands—are used in China, their rugs still have quite a distinctive and different sense of design. Chinese patterns and colors have traditionally been more overtly symbolic than those of other countries. However, while the classic patterns are still used in modern Chinese weaving, their symbolic meanings are no longer important (PLATES XLIII, XLIV, XLVII, and LX). Today, designs that were originally Buddhist or Taoist emblems are reproduced purely as decorations, as are the stylized Chinese ideographs and the traditional dragon, horse, and lotus flower patterns (page 99).

In addition to the common use of classic design elements, certain basic overall patterns are also seen in many weaving areas, and executed in many styles. For example, the garden carpet represents a formal garden and consists of a series of squares or rectangles, each containing an individual design. These show outdoor scenes such as trees, flowers, birds in branches, and fish in pools (PLATES XII, XXXIV). Carpets are also produced in the so-called hunting design that features animals and hunters, or men engaged in combat. The tree of life is another familiar pattern (PLATE XXVIII). Many weavers also produce pictorial rugs that show famous figures from history and folklore or familiar landscapes. And, to give the West its due, there's even a common style inspired by the Aubusson and Savonnerie rugs that were first produced in France in the seventeenth century. This is a floral design that consists of a medallion, an open field, and a complex, broken floral border (PLATE XLI).

Perhaps the most common overall design is the prayer rug. This type of design is very easy to recognize because it has an asymmetrical field that contains an arch (or mihrab) or a similar shape that comes to a point at one end (PLATE XXXVII). These rugs represent the prayer niches used by faithful Moslems in a mosque, and images of the religious articles associated with Islamic worship—lamps, ewers, and combs, to name just a few—are often woven into the field of the rug. Sometimes one long, thin rug will have a row of niches, and then it's known as a saph (PLATE XXXV). In addition, many rugs are worked in a double prayer pattern with niches at both ends of the field (PLATE XXXVIII).

Prayer rugs are produced throughout the Islamic world, but the shapes and sizes of the niches can vary a great deal, depending on the traditions of the area where the rug was made or the tribal background of the weaver. However, contrary to popular belief, it's very rare for any rug with this design to have actually been used in prayer.

It's not hard to see, even from this very brief discussion, that studying the designs used in Oriental rugs, tracing their origins and adaptations, can be a fascinating and complex pursuit. It's important to remember, though, that while symbolism may have been important to the weavers of the past, today's rug designers don't restrict themselves to the traditional guidelines. Generally speaking, neither the colors nor the patterns of today's rugs hold any obscure, secret meaning—if, in fact, they ever did. The main point for you to keep in mind is that the names of the designs and their origins aren't as important as the skill with which those designs are executed.

Don't be unduly impressed by the old adage that rug weavers purposely include imperfections because "only God can make something that's perfect." In modern rugs, obvious flaws in patterns are just that—flaws. On the other hand, with so many hundreds of thousands of knots in each rug, it's inevitable that there will be a few irregularities, and even serious problems in design can occasionally have charming results. However, this is always a matter of taste. You must make this kind of decision yourself, without being influenced by the explanations or preferences of a dealer. All in all, though, when you're buying your first rug it's probably a good idea to buy as perfect a rug as possible.

We'll talk more about how to evaluate the quality of a rug in Chapter V, but before you get down to the specifics be sure to give yourself a chance to see the rug for what it is. Look at its design simply as an arrangement of shapes that are woven in various colors to achieve an overall effect. Don't think about names and styles and symbols. Just look at the colors and shapes; see how well balanced and detailed they are. Remember that the elements of a design are really just arranged to have a pleasing effect. Then ask yourself the obvious question—do you like what you see?

SIZE

When you're considering the size of an Oriental rug, you have to work with two basic factors: the general sizes and shapes in which Oriental rugs are made and the specific size you think you need.

You'll remember from our discussion of the weaving process that a rug can be no wider than the width of the loom on which it's made. It should be obvious, then, that nomadic rugs—made on smaller, more primitive looms—tend to be narrow and that wide rugs are normally made in workshops or factories. The only exception to this rule is the kilim, or flat-woven rug, which is often formed by sewing pieces together lengthwise.

The length of a rug is also dependent on the type of loom on which it's made. As we've seen, there's almost no limit to the length that can be produced on a roller loom, but a regular loom can only yield a length that's less than double the space between the upper and lower support bars.

Another limitation on the size of rugs is a traditional one. In the past, Persian rugs were woven in a set range of sizes, based in part on the way they were arranged in a room. It was the custom to cover a floor not with one large rug but with several smaller ones of various sizes, a practice that made it easier to replace a rug or to move rugs from room to room. In the traditional arrangement of Persian rugs, each had a particular name. For example, a "dozar" was a large rug measuring roughly 6½ feet by 4½ feet, while a "mat" would be 5 or 6 feet square. This scheme of naming the sizes of rugs was also the custom in Turkey.

Both Persian and Turkish size names were often used by rug dealers in the past, but today they're usually abandoned in favor of more precise measurements. However, if you should happen to come across one or another of these terms, you'll find their dimensions listed in the Glossary.

In addition to the traditional sizes, you may also find a few unusual sizes and shapes that have been inspired by the weavers' nomadic heritage. The most common are saddle and tent bags. Today, these are usually stuffed and made into pillows or used as mats or decorative wall-hangings.

Occasionally, you'll also run across round rugs—small pieces from Tabriz and Nain; slightly larger ones, again from Nain; and small room sizes from Kerman. However, these are very few and far between. One reason for the limited selection of round rugs is the relative difficulty involved in designing and weaving them. Nevertheless, a number of Indian rugs are available in round and even oval shapes; the French medallion style of open-field, floral rug is particularly suited to this kind of adaptation. (Incidentally, it may interest you to know that although round and oval rugs are woven on a regular loom, because of the special demands of the shape there can't be a fringe on the sides of these pieces. This has to be added after the rug is removed from the frame.)

Although it's theoretically possible to weave practically any shape, the vast majority of rugs are rectangular. By and large, your shopping will be easier if you simply expect an Oriental rug to have a length—from one fringed end to the other—that's longer than its width. (By the way, you'll notice that throughout this book, when the dimensions of a rug are listed, the length is always given first.) A few pieces *are* woven with the width greater than the length, but these are quite rare.

Over the years, the traditional sizes of Oriental rugs have been altered somewhat to meet the demands of the Western market. Before World War II, when the United States was the major importer of rugs, sizes such as 5 by 3, 6 by 4, 9 by 6, 10 by 8, 12 by 9, and 14 by 10 were all common. Today, because of the dominance of the European market, many rugs (especially those from Iran) come in sizes more popular on the Continent—9 by 5, 10 by 7, and 12 by 8.

In addition, certain weaving areas continue to produce only a limited range of sizes. This standard range of sizes is determined not only by the traditions of each particular area, but also by simple economic reality. Because of today's relatively higher production costs, the selection of sizes is often limited to the ones that are calculated to sell quickly. This keeps the weaver's investment in inventory to a minimum—and by keeping a loom set up for one size of rug, he's able to save time and give his loom the most possible use. It's now quite difficult to find very large rugs because they tie up a loom for too long a period of time and they don't have the ready sales prospects that smaller rugs have.

Standard size ranges can vary from one country to another, and within a country from one weaving area to another. A knowledgeable dealer will be able to give you precise information on the range of sizes produced in a particular region or country. In general, however, you should know that rugs from Iran may be available only in a small range of sizes, depending on the district. Sometimes they're available in only one size. Most Turkish rugs exported to the United States are small, as are most Russian rugs. And rugs from Pakistan may or may not be available in a range of sizes, depending on the pattern. On the other hand, different sizes of rugs in certain basic designs are available from India, China, and Romania. These rugs come in a great range of sizes, albeit standard ones. So the 9 by 6 rug you see and like may very well be found almost identically in a 12 by 9, or perhaps even an 18 by 12. Unusual sizes can often be made to order by modifying a pattern in one of these basic designs, and round and oval rugs are also available.

However, you should be aware that programmed sizes are

available only in a limited number of designs because only certain patterns lend themselves to this kind of adaptation. A small, repeated pattern can be used in a number of sizes, whereas a larger or more intricate design may suffer from too much distortion when it's expanded to fit the proportions of a larger rug. And reducing an intricate pattern may be impossible because there simply won't be enough knots to reproduce all the elements of the design in a smaller size. Even when smaller patterns are used, there will still be slight variations in detailing, especially between very small pieces and their larger counterparts. In other words, there can never be total flexibility in adapting patterns—for the simple reason that while the size of the design is changing, the number of knots per square inch remains the same. This means that curving lines may be distorted, or that some details may have to be eliminated in order to weave a pattern in several different sizes of equal quality. This is why smaller rugs tend to be more finely made; in order to be more attractive, they must have more detail—so they must have more knots.

When you're dealing with all the variables that influence what sizes of rugs are on the market, you can sometimes lose track of your basic concern—determining what size rug *you* need. To do this, start by taking into account not only the size of the room, but how it's used. Sketch out the dimensions of the room, using the planning sheets in the Appendix, remembering to show the shape and position of the furniture, and the traffic patterns.

As a general rule, common sense dictates that you buy the smallest rug that will do the job. There are two good reasons for this: first, it reduces the cost, and second, since there are more small rugs on the market than large ones, the smaller the rug you can use the more rugs you'll have to choose from. Even so, you may still have to be somewhat flexible. The standard sizes that are now being imported are, as we've seen, dictated by European rather than American tastes. Unfortunately, these shapes don't always correspond with the way modern American homes are being built; the trend here is toward rooms that are somewhat more square than those in Europe. And if you have an older home, with narrower rooms than those in Europe, you may have just the opposite problem, since the width of rugs generally increases with their length.

However, the situation isn't as bleak as it might seem. After all, there's tremendous flexibility and variety in today's lifestyles, and as a result there's much more freedom exercised in decorating. This means that there can be a lot of latitude in terms of what size rug is right for a room. If you find a rug that you like in a particular size that doesn't initially appear to be workable, you can often rearrange the layout of the room to adapt to the new size. Instead of using a large rug under several pieces of furniture you could use a smaller rug in front of one of them; or you could use several smaller rugs.

The trick is to be flexible when you're considering different sizes of rugs—and to use some common sense. Determine your color preference first, and then adapt your design and size preferences to it. By consulting the directory in Chapter VIII, you'll be able to determine the general range of sizes that are available in each type of rug. Decide which sizes might suit your needs and then be realistic about your options. Don't torture yourself or brutalize a dealer by insisting on a size that isn't made or a size that's so unusual that there's little or no hope of locating it. Look at all the possibilities and keep an open mind—and you're likely to find that the size of your new rug won't be a problem at all.

CHAPTER V

SELECTING A RUG

 OVER THE CENTURIES, ORIENTAL RUGS HAVE been elevated from a purely utilitarian function to the level of art. But, unlike other art, Oriental rugs can't just be beautiful to look at; they must also be functional. In other words, if they're to keep their beauty through years of wear they must meet certain standards of quality.

As you would expect, the quality of Oriental rugs can vary tremendously. At the lower end of the scale, you'll find pieces with fuzzy, distorted designs and garish colors—rugs so poorly made that they only appeal to buyers who look at nothing but the price tag. This kind of shoddy merchandise is difficult to disguise, even to someone who's only begun shopping for an Oriental. However, once this level of goods is left behind, the first-time buyer is often unsure of how to judge a variety of rugs, how to compare them, and how to determine their quality. After all, a certain amount of variation, and even slight irregularities, are the hallmark of a handmade rug—but where should you draw the line between what's acceptable and what isn't? And how should you weigh these standards of quality against the limitations that might be imposed by your budget?

It helps to start off by having an understanding of all the factors that determine the price of a rug. Basically, this begins with the cost of materials, labor, and handling. Other factors that come into play are the size of the rug, the quality of the pile, the workmanship involved, the quality of the rug's warp and weft, and the density of the weave. In addition, the area where the rug was made can also have an influence on its price. Some countries, and some weaving districts within those countries, have better reputations than others—so that even if all the other factors are relatively equal, the prices of rugs from these areas will be higher than those of similar ones from other areas.

Obviously, your personal needs and preferences will have a lot to do with how you weigh all these variables, but you can't expect to make the right choice unless you can assess at least some features of a rug for yourself. It's essential that you carry out a careful inspection of every rug you're interested in, and that you consider certain standards of workmanship when you do. Remember that an Oriental rug has been handled thousands of times before you buy it, and it should be able to stand up to many more years of handling and wear after you buy it.

THE INITIAL INSPECTION

When you choose an Oriental rug, your first consideration is simply an aesthetic one—whether or not you like the rug. Start out by looking at rugs in all the basic colors. Don't be afraid to ask the dealer to show you a number of rugs, and don't worry about the price tags or try to remember all the names. Just look at the colors and patterns and gradually weed out the ones you don't like. Once you've established your preferences, you can always make substitutions within a basic group of colors and styles to satisfy the needs of your budget.

If you've visited any other stores, it will help everyone if you tell the dealer what rugs you've already seen—mention which ones you liked or disliked. Don't be embarrassed to admit that you've been shopping around; it will always be to your advantage, and it will enable you and the dealer to save a lot of time and trouble. It also helps to tell the dealer where the rug will be used, and to provide any information on colors and sizes that might help narrow down your choices. Finally, as a dealer, let me make one final plea—don't bring officious friends with you when you shop. You need to follow your own tastes when you're picking out a rug. You also need to concentrate, so don't tax your children's patience by bringing them along when you know they may become restless.

Obviously, when you're narrowing down your choices of color and pattern you shouldn't expect or need to make a minute inspection of every rug you see. However, once you've determined that you could be happy living with a particular rug, then it's time to look at it more carefully.

Have the rug you're considering spread out flat on the floor, under lighting that isn't too soft or too bright. Look at the design on the rug's field and make sure that the pattern is reasonably symmetrical. An easy way to check this is to fold the rug in half lengthwise and match the two layers for length—you should be able to see exactly half of the central design. Repeat the same process by folding the rug across the width.

Next, spread the rug out flat and look at the individual elements of the design. If there's a medallion, is it fairly centered? If there are vertical and horizontal lines that are meant to be straight, are they in fact straight? Check the individual elements of the overall design; if they're repeated, are they uniform? Are corresponding design elements and open spaces in the pattern the same size and shape? Are they well-balanced? There's no reason for negative answers to any of these questions, despite what a salesman may say. Symmetry is basic to the design of most Oriental rugs, and the lack of it is simply the result of poor workmanship.

Next, look at the colors used in the rug. Are they deep and rich? Do they have a luster or are they dull? And don't forget to look at your selection from each end. You'll remember from our discussion of the weaving process that pile rugs have a certain nap that's created when the weaver pulls the knots down toward him as he works. You'll notice that when the rug is seen from the direction in which it was woven, its colors will look darker and richer and the designs will be more distinctive.

Also pay careful attention to the lighter colors in the rug. Look at the edges of these areas to make sure that none of the adjoining darker colors have run. Sometimes a slight bit of "fugitive" color is acceptable, but if it's any more serious the rug should be put aside.

Compare individual colors in different parts of the rug; there shouldn't be any significant variations. On the other hand, color changes along a horizontal line (abrash) are often seen in nomadic rugs, and if they're gradual, they're not usually considered a problem. However, if the color change is sharp, it should be reason enough to reject the rug.

Once you've inspected the colors and the pattern, step back and look at the whole rug. Does it lie flat? Does it have a reasonably regular shape? Some rugs can be quite crooked, with irregular, undulating sides; others tend to be narrower in the middle than at the ends; and still others can be narrower at one end. All these irregularities are caused when the weaver pulls the wefts tighter in some spots than others. Some rugs are also misshapen because the manufacturer simply hasn't been careful with them. You shouldn't be asked to pay the full price for any of these rugs.

Keep in mind, however, that some bumps or wrinkles are the result of baling when the rugs are in transport or creasing while they're in storage. As long as they aren't too extreme, these kinds of bumps and wrinkles, as well as minor irregularities in shape, can be corrected by blocking and stretching. A full-service dealer will be able to accept this responsibility.

Finally, you should make sure that the foundation and pile of a new rug are free of damage that might have occurred during shipping. Look for obvious repairs or for discoloration that may have been caused by water. Carefully fold the rug in the area you think may be damaged and listen for a cracking sound.

A CLOSER LOOK

When you look at rugs, they're usually stacked, with each rug lying face up. However, it's very important to turn over at least a part of any rug you're interested in. If you watch a dealer buying rugs you'll notice that one of the first things he does when he's looking at a rug is to kick over one of the corners. This isn't just a meaningless routine, the way someone who's shopping for a car might kick one of the tires. The fact is that a dealer can usually pick out the rug he wants from a stack of pieces, even though only a portion of the back is visible. That's because the reverse side tells a lot about the rug's character. A dealer will rely on the weave and the structure as they're revealed on the back of the rug when he's identifying its source. Since it's formed out of sight, this side often reveals the idiosyncracies of the weaver and the region.

By looking at the back of the rug, you can easily determine the number of knots and the distance between the rows—and these will tell how fine and close the weaving is. The back of the rug also gives you a clear indication of how uniform the pattern is.

When you're counting the knots on the back of a rug, the usual practice is to measure how many there are in a square inch. Naturally, you can get a more accurate estimate by counting the knots in several different places and then averaging the results. The purpose of this knot counting is to make comparisons between various rugs, and it works best when you're considering several rugs from one particular area. Comparisons of knot counts can be used only in a very general way with rugs from different weaving centers because other factors—such as the feel of the pile material, the quality of the dyes, and the overall construction—must be taken into account when you're dealing with rugs that weren't made in the same locale. We'll go into the range of qualities you'll find within certain weaving areas in Chapters VII and VIII; for the moment, just learn how to count knots.

First, make sure you know what type of knot has been used in the rug. To do this, just crack open the face of the rug and isolate an individual knot. Turn back to Chapter II, and use the drawings on page 68 as a reference. If a collar of wool encircles the ends of the pile thread so that it can't be separated, the knot is Turkish. If you *are* able to separate the two ends of the pile yarn, you'll find that the collar only surrounds one side of the knot—so the knot is Persian.

To count Persian knots, you simply add up the number of loops or bumps within one inch, vertically and horizontally, on the back of the rug and then multiply them. The same process goes for the Turkish knot, but you must be careful in this case not to mistake one knot for two, or two for one (which happens when the warps are fully stacked, one directly on top of the other).

Sometimes when you're making comparisons between rugs, the difference in the fineness of the weaves may be obvious—but often it may not. In this case, it helps to remember a very general rule of thumb: the finer the fringe, the finer the rug.

The thickness of the wefts is also a factor because it affects the flexibility of a rug. For example, pieces with a relatively low knot count will feel firm if they've been woven with heavy wefts. This type of wefting doesn't add to the durability of the rug—the knot count is still a much surer guide.

Another obvious way to check the quality of the rug is to see how much of the foundation is visible on the back of the rug. Warps (except, of course, at the fringes) are not normally visible unless the rug is single-wefted. As for the wefts, the more of these threads that you can see, the coarser the rug will be.

When you're dealing with flat-woven Orientals, obviously the process of inspecting the weave is a bit different: you can determine the fineness of kilim rugs by counting the number of warp threads in a given section of the rug and the number of rows of the pattern-forming weft threads in the same section.

Aside from giving you an idea of the fineness of the weave, a look at the back of the rug will also help you to spot any uneven weaving techniques and any damage that may have been repaired. These can be very difficult to see from the front of the carpet. Although it's not uncommon to find repairs in older rugs, when you're buying a new rug there shouldn't be any obvious repairs or patches. In fact, there should never be anything, except perhaps an occasional label, sewn on the back of the new carpet. The only exception to this rule is the practice of sewing leather or cardboard strips along the sides of the heavy, finely woven pieces; this is done to keep the edges from curling.

The sides, or selvedge edges, should also be examined from

the back of the rug. These must be tightly and evenly wound with what looks like a buttonhole stitch. During the weaving, the wefts are passed across the rug and incorporated into the selvedges. However, it's a common practice today to weave two narrow rugs side by side on a single wide loom. The weft threads are passed across the entire width of the loom, through both rugs, and when they're removed from the loom, the two carpets are slit apart, cutting the wefts. A prefabricated selvedge is then sewn onto the exposed raw edge, or it's wrapped by overcasting. It's quite rare for the two edges to match exactly. If this is the case with the rug you're considering, make sure that the edge is firmly secured to the body of the carpet so that the severed wefts will be strengthened and protected. And don't be alarmed if you find extra wefts inserted for a short distance at intervals along the edges. These are intended to stiffen the sides and protect them.

Once you've examined the selvedges, have a close look at the fringes. Make sure they're knotted in groups or that they're sewn in by overcasting, which secures each pair along the way. Then compare the fringes at one end of the rug with the fringes at the other—because they may not be the same. Many rugs have only a webbing at the starting end, but are fringed at the opposite end. If you want the ends to match, the webbing may be removed by unraveling the wefts, and then it can be overcast to form a fringe. By the same token, if the original fringes on the rug aren't of equal length, they can be trimmed.

You'll find that the fringes on small rugs are often much too short. This happens when several rugs are woven end to end from the bottom to the top of a large loom, a practice that enables a weaver to produce several rugs without resetting the warps on the loom. Sometimes the weaver fails to leave enough unwoven warps between the rugs, and this results in rugs with very short fringes, or even no fringes at all.

When you've finished looking at the fringes, check the pile by rubbing your hand over the surface of the rug. The height should be the same from one end to the other. If you can feel undulations in the pile, then it's likely that the rug hasn't been sheared properly. If the unevenness isn't too great, it may be something you can live with—but you're the only one who can decide this. On the other hand, excessive and harsh washing during the finishing process, which can also make the pile irregular and sparse, is usually a more serious matter. It should be reason enough to reject a rug.

When you're checking the pile, it's important to remember that the height of the pile isn't a reliable gauge of the rug's quality —that's determined by the fineness of the weave, along with the density and quality of the pile materials. Coarse yarns may produce a high, thick pile, but they simply can't be used to weave delicate patterns. After all, the thicker the yarn, the fewer stitches it takes to fill up each square inch of the rug.

Remember to check the way the pile fiber feels. If it's wool, is it smooth, yet tough, or does it feel dry and brittle? Good wool has sheen, strength, and elasticity. There's a common misconception that softer wool is better wool, but the fact is that softer wool doesn't wear well, tends to soil quickly, and doesn't respond to cleaning as well as tough, wiry wool that springs back after it's been pressed down. When this kind of wool is woven closely, the ends of the fibers take the brunt of the wear and the sides of the fibers are protected. Over the years the pile wears away more gradually and the foundation receives more protection.

As you're inspecting the pile, you may also notice a few white threads mixed in with the wool or a few knots that seem to be made of white cotton. The former is just a thread that's somehow worked its way into the yarn; the latter is either part of the foundation or a knot where two lengths of the foundation are joined. These white threads are nothing to worry about—the dealer can simply clip them off for you.

Finally, spend a moment or two to make sure that the pile of the rug doesn't seem dirty. Rugs are made under less than sterile conditions, and they have to be cleaned to remove dirt and odors. If the rug you're looking at is clean, it won't have any noticeable smell.

Most of the rugs exported to the United States have been cleaned and many of them have been chemically washed. However, it's not uncommon to find pieces that haven't been touched, and in this case the cleaning becomes the dealer's responsibility.

You shouldn't be asked to pay for this; all rugs should be cleaned before they're sold.

If all this advice makes inspecting a rug sound like a lot of trouble, believe me, it's really not. After all, the entire rug is right in front of you. There are few hidden parts—and no moving ones! While there *are* some unscrupulous practices that may fool you— if, for instance, the weaver has inserted heavy wefts to give the appearance of body to a rug—it's also true that many basic elements, such as the knot count, simply can't be camouflaged. And if you're worried about how much time it may take to look at a number of rugs, or if you're nervous about performing your inspection in front of a dealer, just relax. Remember, if you take advantage of the dealer's offer of home trial, you can do most of the examination in the privacy of your own home, and at your own pace.

A Few Words on Machinemade Rugs

Many of the traditional designs found in Oriental rugs have been reproduced by machine in both the United States and Europe. As some classic handmade patterns become harder to find—and as all handmade rugs become more expensive—these machinemade copies will become even more common. Of course, my overriding interest is in handmade Orientals, but at the same time I refuse to condemn all of these machinemade copies. Many are well made, and some are even of better quality than the handmade rugs that inspired them—so good, in fact, that a customer in our store, on seeing a classically designed Persian rug, once exclaimed that it must have been copied from a Karastan!

Unlike plain machinemade carpets, some machinemade Orientals retain their resale value. Obviously, only the better rugs fit in this category, and they're by no means inexpensive. These rugs —made on a modified Axminster loom or in the Wilton (Jacquard) manufacturing style—are certainly far superior to the machinemade rugs that are made by printing an Oriental design onto a plain-colored carpet. In fact, they're not even comparable.

By and large, if you have no special feeling or desire for something that's made by hand, you may be just as well off with one of the better machinemade reproductions. Remember, though, that no mechanical process can duplicate the Persian, Turkish, or Spanish knot. No reputable dealer will show you a machinemade carpet and tell you that it's handmade. However, there are a few obvious differences that you should be aware of if you need to make the distinction for yourself. Just follow these steps:

(1) Break open the pile. You won't find any knot (no loop or collar) at the base of the pile of a machinemade rug. (2) Look at the back of the rug. A hand-knotted rug is slightly irregular; it will show only warps if it's single wefted or if it's woven with the Spanish knot. There will never be continuous, straight lines running the length of a handmade carpet, as there are in many machinemade ones. (3) Look at the fringe. Is it part of the basic construction of the rug? In new Oriental rugs (as distinguished from older pieces, which may have been repaired) the fringe is actually a continuation of the warp and is never added to the body of the rug, as is the case with machinemade copies. (4) Look at the selvedges. In handmade Oriental rugs, the side edges, or selvedges, are wrapped by hand. On copies, they're put on by machine.

One final warning: some Chinese-style rugs are machinemade by a method known as tufting. In this technique, a tool that looks like a gun is used to insert the yarns through a prefabricated foundation. From the face, these pieces are often indistinguishable from handmade carpets, even to an expert, but on the back an extra backing made of canvas, jute, or duck will hide the loops, either totally or partially. Remember, if a rug is handmade the loops on the back should be *completely* visible.

CHAPTER VI

TRYING A RUG AT HOME:
A FEW DECORATING
CONSIDERATIONS

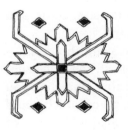TRYING OUT A RUG IN YOUR HOME OR OFFICE HAS distinct advantages, both for you and your rug dealer. For you, this is a time when you'll be able to examine the rug carefully in an unpressured environment. You'll have a chance to look at the rug in daylight and under artificial light, and you'll be able to see how it fits in with your decor and lifestyle. You can also spend as much time as you need to perform the inspection that was outlined in Chapter V. If you notice anything that bothers or confuses you, you'll have an opportunity to discuss it with the dealer before you make a final decision.

At first, you might wonder how home trial can also be advantageous to a dealer, but as soon as you get a rug home you'll see why. The appearance of a handmade Oriental rug will usually enhance, and be enhanced by, its surroundings. You won't be looking at the rug simply as one of many rugs in a showroom; instead, you'll be seeing it with your furniture and your accessories. Obviously, a dealer lets you try a rug at home because he hopes that you won't want to part with it once you see how well it works.

But be fair about all this. Don't take advantage of a home-trial offer unless you're ready to commit yourself and you've carefully narrowed down your choice to a few likely candidates. Above all, treat the borrowed rug with even more respect than you would your own property. After all, you're responsible for it while it's in your home. Finally, don't keep a trial rug for an unreasonable period of time. Allow yourself a few days to live with it and examine it—and then make up your mind.

The ideal time to buy an Oriental rug is before you've selected anything else for a room. There are infinitely more paint colors, wallpaper patterns, and fabrics available than there are Oriental rugs, and building your room around the possibilities that present themselves in an Oriental rug can often yield spectacular results.

However, most rug buyers aren't starting a room from scratch, and the smartest way to determine which rug is right with what you already have is simply to try it out. But before you bring a rug home for trial, take some time to consider the size, color, and general pattern that will work best in your room.

There are no strict guidelines on what size a rug should be—except that it should work with, rather than against, the placement of your furniture. For this reason, you'll probably find that you can choose between a variety of different sizes, all of which could be used in the same room. Once you've determined which one of these sizes you prefer, you'll save yourself a lot of needless frustration if you're still prepared to allow for some latitude, perhaps up to five percent in length or width and ten percent in the total area of the rug.

Obviously, the first step in choosing a size is to think about how much floor space you want to cover, and the different ways you can arrange your furniture to set off the rug. Remember, there's no "one size fits all" in the world of Oriental rugs. However, as obvious as this is, it's the rare customer who comes to see a rug dealer with a scaled floor plan that shows the placement and size of all the furniture in a room. This simple ingredient will make life easier for everyone; it will practically shout out what size rug you should have. So before you do anything else, use the scaling sheets in the Appendix and carefully draw up a floor plan, making sure to include any features of the room that are distinctive, such as a fireplace. To be on the safe side, don't forget to write down the actual dimensions of the room—then even if your drawing is off a bit, you'll still be within the right size range.

Once you've made a floor plan, you can consider the options that are open to you. First, remember that Oriental rugs aren't meant to cover a floor completely. If you want the wall-to-wall feeling, it makes more sense to buy broadloom carpeting and use small Oriental throw rugs as accents on top of it.

If you want to use an Oriental to cover most of the floor space in a room, measure the room's dimensions and then allow eighteen to twenty-four inches of bare floor on all four sides. Then you won't be hiding too much of the border pattern—which is like the frame of a picture—under furniture that's placed against the wall. (By the way, when you're making your calculations, it helps to remember that the depth of the average piece of upholstered furniture is 32 inches.)

This basic scheme of determining the right dimensions for a room-sized rug can be varied slightly to adapt to any distinctive features the room might contain. For example, if there's a fireplace with a hearth that extends into the room, then the rug can be brought flush against it or close to it, leaving an eighteen to twenty-four inch margin on the opposite side of the room. This will help you avoid distorting the room's proportions through the size and shape of your rug. After all, if the fireplace is on one of the longer walls of your room and you leave an eighteen to twenty-four inch margin of floor space between the hearth and the rug, then you'll have to choose a narrower rug—which will further accentuate the length of the room. So if you're positioning a rug near a fireplace, pull it right up against the hearth—and don't worry about the danger of sparks. The wool in the pile of a rug simply doesn't burn that easily.

Another thing to think about is whether you really need a large rug in the first place. Look at the groupings of chairs, tables, or sofas; see if a rug placed in front of or under just one of these groups might not be a better solution. Remember that the place-ment of a rug can be used to define an area. Many large rooms have several distinct functions, and rugs can separate them very nicely. For example, two different rugs can set off a dining area from a living room area, or a study area with a desk from an enter-taining area with a sofa and chairs.

As we've seen, the shape of a rug can also change the propor-tions of a room. Rectangular rugs, or long runners, can lengthen a space, while two different rugs can shorten or subdivide that same space. And a rug that's placed on the bias can also change the way you look at a room.

In addition, it pays to consider the traffic patterns in a room, and how you might want to alter or adapt to them by directing the flow along the width or the length of a rug. For example, walking over the fringed end and along the length of a rug seems to direct people into a particular area, while crossing over the side of a rug sometimes makes people hesitate. This factor is especially impor-tant in areas such as foyers, where the careless placement of a rug could lead visitors in the wrong direction. Even if they don't ac-tually stray into the kitchen or the powder room instead of the liv-ing room, their eyes will have been diverted that way.

The needs of each particular room should also be considered. For example, a dining room rug doesn't need to be any larger than the area taken up when the chairs are pushed out from the table. That's why it's particularly important to know not only the room size but the dimensions of your table and chairs. In addition, you should expect a dining room rug to be quite durable because push-ing the chairs away from and toward the table causes a good deal of stress on the pile fibers—and the situation is made worse by the fact that this punishment is constantly inflicted on the same area of the rug.

The size of a bedroom rug also needs to be selected carefully because the bed may hide a great deal of the carpet. Actually, it's sometimes better to use a number of small pieces around the furni-ture in a bedroom, at the same time taking care to choose sizes large enough so that bare floor and bare feet don't meet!

When you're carpeting a stairway, don't forget the possibilities presented by an Oriental—you'll often find that the rug's patterns take on a striking look when they're seen from such a different perspective. Be sure, though, to buy a very good quality carpet for your stairway and have it installed with the nap facing down the steps. This will ensure that it stands up to all the wear it will be getting.

Of course, it makes sense to consider the wear *any* carpet will be bearing. Keep in mind the fact that merely walking across a rug doesn't cause as much wear as sitting in a particular area and digging in the heels of your shoes. This is why a den, a study, or a library—any area where people will be sitting—should have a sturdy rug. In other words, don't buy something inexpensive for a high-traffic area. You may pay more for a better quality rug, but it will last much longer, and look better longer.

Once you've considered the needs of the room, you should also consider the needs of the rug. The edges of rugs are their weakest parts, and you should avoid any placement where normal traffic would expose them to constant use. A rug shouldn't end within an arch or a doorway, nor should there be bare floor between a rug and a piece of furniture that's used for seating. If this happens, the edge of the rug will wear prematurely, and you'll also find that people will always be tripping over it.

As if this isn't enough to consider, you must also remember that, because of the technique of knotting, rugs have a direction—that is, a lay of the pile or nap. This will always feel smooth towards the end where the weaving was begun. When the rug is seen from this end, the pile takes on a darker, richer look, and the pattern is more distinct because less light is reflected off the surface. Keep this in mind when you're considering the placement of a rug—but don't forget that the rug will have to be reversed periodically to even out the wear.

So far, we've concentrated on the size and placement of your new rug, mainly because color and design are so much more dependent on your own personal taste. However, there are a few general color and design considerations you should keep in mind.

113

Although your choice of color will be dependent on the other furnishings in the room, you'll probably have a variety of shades to work with. If you have any of the paint that was used on the walls, dab a bit on a small piece of cardboard and bring it with you when you shop. And if you can bring a sample of the fabric from any upholstered furniture, that will help guide your choices too.

By selecting carefully, you'll set the basic tone of a given room through the use of either cool or warm colors. Remember too that a light rug enlarges a room, while a darker one seems to reduce its dimensions. And don't forget the practical aspect of picking out your colors. A pastel rug might be fine for a bedroom or a room that isn't used a great deal—but it wouldn't be very smart to put such a rug in the most heavily traveled part of your living room or at the front door.

In the same way, you should consider the basic type of design that's best suited to your furniture and your style of living. Oriental rugs can blend with a variety of decorating styles—from antiques to modern—but you ought to keep the proportions of a particular rug's design in mind. For example, if you like a spare, uncluttered look and haven't a great deal of furniture, a medallion rug would be an ideal choice—but the same rug would be lost if you have a lot of furniture hiding the medallion. This is often the case in a dining room or a bedroom, and in these rooms an all-over design may work much better.

The most important consideration, though, is that you put your new Oriental rug where you'll enjoy it the most. After all, if you're going to buy a fine handmade carpet, you should expect it to wear well, and you should put it where you—and everyone who visits your home—can see and admire it.

CHAPTER VII

A BRIEF TOUR OF THE RUG-PRODUCING COUNTRIES

ALTHOUGH IT SEEMS FAIRLY ARBITRARY, THE traditional practice of grouping rugs according to their country of origin still makes sense, simply because most rugs from a particular area do in fact have certain basic similarities. And in the case of some countries, such as Romania and China, where the rug industry is regulated by the central government, this is really the only logical way the country's rugs, from whatever region, can be discussed.

It's also true, however, that certain styles and designs that may have originated in one country or among one group of people have, over the years, been adopted by weavers in other areas and are now being produced in many countries throughout the world. For this reason, we'll save a detailed discussion of rug types for the directory in Chapter VIII and concentrate here on a much more general overview of the rug industry, past and present, in each of the major producing countries.

115

IRAN

To many people, the terms "Persian rug" and "Oriental rug" are practically interchangeable—and with good reason. The Persian empire was one of the oldest and most powerful in the Middle East, and weaving was always an important part of its artistic tradition. It's not surprising, then, that the fifteenth and sixteenth centuries, the period when Persian culture reached its peak under the Safavid dynasty, should also be known as the golden age of Oriental rugmaking.

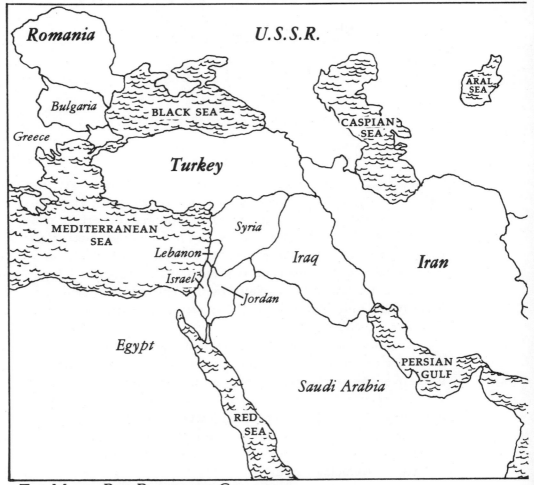

THE MAJOR RUG-PRODUCING COUNTRIES

A Brief Tour of the Rug-Producing Countries

The Safavid shahs were great patrons of the arts, and they brought skilled craftsmen from all over the empire to their capital at Isfahan. There the court artisans produced rugs that were quite unlike the geometrically designed carpets found in other Islamic countries. These new rugs had elegant, intricately curving designs, and they were woven with the finest materials in the most precise detail. The magnificent court rugs made for the Safavid shahs represent the height of the art of weaving; in fact, they set the standards of workmanship and design that are still used to judge the finest Oriental rugs.

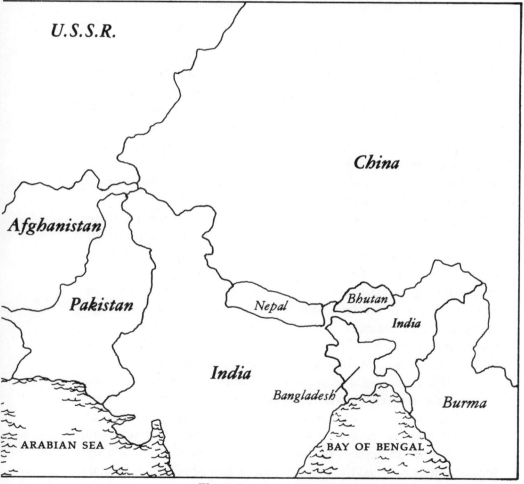

The major rug-producing countries are labeled in **bold** type.

Today, the Persian empire is long gone, and its weaving tradition is only one of several that survive in Iran. The country's population includes a number of different ethnic groups, and the rugs they produce can range from unsophisticated nomadic pieces to finely detailed workshop carpets that are descendants of the Safavid court rugs.

Modern Iranian rug production can be divided into three different categories. The smallest percentage of the total comes from nomadic tribes and their sedentary kinsmen, who live in small farming villages. These nomads and villagers don't rely on weaving for their livelihood and their rugs are generally inexpensive or moderately priced, primarily because they're not as sophisticated or as finely knotted as most other Iranian rugs.

Although nomad and village weavers use traditional designs, it would be naive to think that they've escaped the influence of the commercial marketplace. It's really only a matter of degree, since the nomad and village weavers, just like their counterparts in the city, are interested in getting the best profit from their looms. Generally, this means that they're less likely to experiment, that they'll stick to a basic design that they know will sell. Nevertheless, there will still be minor variations in design from rug to rug; very few will look exactly the same.

Since the nomad and village looms are more primitive, these weavers produce only small rugs; in addition, their selection of materials is usually limited to whatever is available in the area. When nomad and village rugs are completed, they're taken to a central depository in one of the nearby towns or cities. There the rugs are sheared, washed, and sold to a buyer or an exporter. Nomad and village rugs can vary a good deal in the fineness, or coarseness, of the weaving, mainly because the only quality control is whether or not the market will accept their goods.

Another more common form of Iranian rug production involves an entrepreneur who contracts carpets on speculation by providing weavers with enough money to cover the cost of materials and labor. The weaver makes the basic decisions on what patterns and colors to use, but these choices are bound by local traditions. When the contract rugs are finished, the financial backer gathers them up and sells them, usually to shopkeepers in the bazaars. Because no strict specifications are laid down, these pieces can and do vary a great deal in quality.

This is definitely not the case with the large resident companies that are responsible for the majority of Iran's rug production. These firms have standing orders from foreign traders to export certain types and quantities of rugs, which are made in workrooms that usually contain many looms. These rug manufacturers subsidize their weaving and fully control it, dictating all the specifications of the rugs, including the color and the size. Obviously, this form of production is much more efficient than nomad or speculative weaving, and it means that the quality of workroom, or "factory," rugs can be much more consistent.

Whether they're made in an isolated village or in a city workshop, Iranian rugs are usually named after the town or district in or near which they're produced or collected. Each area has its traditional basic patterns, executed in a standard palette of colors, often using some distinctive weaving technique. Except for the nomadic pieces, which are less sophisticated, the designs found in Iranian rugs generally reflect the passion for detail—the intricate interplay of lines and repeated patterns—that's also found in Iranian painting, tiles, and calligraphy. However, Iranian weavers certainly aren't averse to making changes to suit the tastes of their foreign customers. Today, some Iranian weavers are substituting light colors and earth tones for the traditional primary colors, and adapting some of the classic designs and sizes.

If you have a knowledge of all the characteristics—colors, designs, materials, weaving technique—that are found in each region, you'll be able to identify the precise source of most Iranian rugs. However, the matter becomes complicated by the fact that most Iranian designs have been reproduced in other countries throughout the world. You'll find detailed descriptions of the traditional Iranian patterns, and information on foreign copies, in the directory of rug types in the next chapter.

As is the case with all Oriental rugs, Iranian rugs must be considered not only in terms of design, but also in terms of the quality of the weaving, which can vary tremendously within a given area.

It isn't enough simply to know where a rug has been made—you must also make a careful inspection of the rug itself and compare it with other rugs from the same area.

In general, the materials used in Iranian rugs—like the colors and designs—are constant within each weaving district. In general, the majority of Iranian rugs have wool pile on a cotton foundation, but you'll also find coarser rugs woven on wool foundations in the areas where nomadic traditions are still maintained, as well as very fine pieces woven on silk and linen in the towns around Nain, Isfahan, and Qum. In Qum, you can find wool pile rugs with accents of silk (usually outlining or highlighting designs), silk pile rugs worked on silk and cotton foundations, and rugs made entirely of silk. In Isfahan, silk is sometimes used for the warps, while in Nain it's frequently used in outlining.

As you might expect, most Iranian rugs are made with Persian knots. However, you'll find that rugs from the Azerbaijan district, in the northwestern part of the country near the Russian border, are woven with Turkish knots. The weavers in this area use a small hook to work the pile threads into the foundations, a technique that makes it impossible to tie Persian knots.

Iranian rugs can range tremendously in price, but they're generally more expensive than rugs of comparable quality from other areas. This is due to the fact that the country's labor and production costs have risen dramatically. In addition, child labor laws, compulsory education, and opportunities for higher paying employment in the cities have substantially reduced the rug industry's work force. And the uncertain political climate in Iran hasn't helped the situation. Statistics show that there's been a sharp decline in Iranian rug production over the last twenty years. Naturally, this means that the prices for those that reach the marketplace have risen dramatically, and will continue to do so. Obviously, at some point Iranian rugs will become too expensive for most of the buying public, and a great weaving tradition may well end. Even now, it's being seriously threatened by the upsurge in rug production in other countries. However, despite the dismal prospects for the future, Iranian rugs continue to be the best choice for buyers who are interested in "investing" in Orientals.

A Brief Tour of the Rug-Producing Countries

TURKEY

Rug weaving was probably brought to Turkey by the Seljuks, a nomadic people from Central Asia who appeared in the region in the eleventh century and had conquered it by the thirteenth. The Seljuks were soon threatened by other Central Asian invaders, the Ottomans, whose empire reached its greatest strength in the fifteenth and sixteenth centuries and lingered on into the twentieth. Rugs from the Ottoman Empire were imported into Europe by Italian traders in the late Middle Ages, and until the seventeenth century, when Persian rugs began to appear, Oriental rugs were, to most Europeans, simply "Turkey carpets."

During the nineteenth and early twentieth centuries, a large number of Turkish rugs were exported to the United States. These were often known as Smyrna carpets, since they were collected and exported from that city. Unfortunately, the rug trade was disrupted during and after the First World War, and in these years the destruction of the Greek and Armenian populations, which were extremely important to the weaving industry, had a crippling effect on Turkish rug production. But today, after decades of decline, Turkey has once again become an important exporter of rugs, primarily due to the government's efforts to encourage weaving as a cottage industry. State-run weaving schools have been established in an effort to reduce rural poverty and provide a surer source of foreign exchange—and in the process, weaving itself has become much more uniform throughout the country.

Historically, Turkish methods of producing rugs are similar to those used in Iran. Less sophisticated traditional patterns are woven by nomads and villagers, while more formal styles are created in workshops or factories. However, unlike in Iran, much of the weaving in Turkey is done as a cottage industry, produced by Turkey's vast rural populace, usually on a part-time basis. These rugs tend to be rather small because they're woven by women and girls in their homes, or in small workshops containing several looms. However, since the rugs are bought as piecework (the weavers are paid by the knot) rather than on speculation, the contract buyers are able to exert strict control over color and design.

This factor is especially important in rugs earmarked for the United States because the traditional bright red and blue colors in Turkish rugs haven't been popular in America.

The willingness of Turkish contractors to produce rugs in softer tones has done a great deal to revive the popularity of Turkish rugs in America. The Turkish weaving industry has also shown an interest in producing a range of traditional designs. Today, modern representations of classic Turkish, Iranian, and Caucasian patterns are all appearing on the international market.

Most of the traditional Turkish styles are named for the city or region in which they were first made; the major ones are described in the directory in the following chapter. In general, you'll find that even the most sophisticated Turkish designs rarely include depictions of men or animals. Unlike the Iranians, the Sunnite Moslems of Turkey still observe the Koran's injunction against portraying these figures. The influence of these religious beliefs can also be seen in the large number of prayer rugs produced in Turkey.

Turkish rugs are generally woven on foundations of either cotton or wool, and the pile is usually made of good quality wool. The pile yarns are dyed with reliable German chrome dyes in a wide range of colorfast shades. Silk or mercerized cotton is also occasionally used for both the pile and the foundation. In fact, the silk rugs made in Hereke can be among the finest in the world, and some of these pieces can contain silver and gold threads. There is also a considerable amount of flat, or kilim, weaving done in Turkey (PLATE XXXII).

Turkish rug producers are finding more markets every year, but their exports to the United States are still fairly limited. Today, rugs come to America from only a few of the hundreds of weaving areas in the country, mainly because the colors, designs, and sizes of rugs made in many of these regions are still tailored to meet the demand from European countries, particularly Germany. In fact, the largest producing center in Turkey, Isparta, exports only a very small number of rugs to the United States.

New Turkish rugs that do reach the American market tend to be in smaller sizes, and in classic designs. Although the prices of these rugs remain comparatively high, the initial expense can be justified somewhat by the fact that good quality Turkish rugs show signs of holding their investment value.

INDIA

Pile weaving came to northern India in the sixteenth century, in the wake of the Mogul conquest. The Moguls were Moslems who had been thoroughly influenced by Persian culture, and they brought all its trappings with them to their new homeland. The carpet factories established by the Mogul emperors were staffed by Persian weavers who trained native craftsmen to produce faithful copies of Persian designs, along with variations of classic patterns, including all-over designs featuring scrolling leaves and vines and large, finely drawn flowers.

After the decline of the Moguls and the rise of British India, rug weaving, which had been carried out to satisfy the special needs of the Mogul aristocracy, lost a good deal of its vitality. However, at the end of the nineteenth century, the weaving trade was reorganized to meet the demands of the European market, and large numbers of rugs began to be exported. Many of these rugs were quite crudely woven, in simple, garishly colored patterns, using inferior materials. Naturally, they were also very inexpensive. These poorly made rugs continued to be produced in great numbers until well after the Second World War, and they had a damaging effect on the reputation of India's rug industry. Fortunately, Indian manufacturers recognized this situation and in recent years they've made great strides in improving the quality of their rugs. In many respects, Indian weaving has come full circle, and the trend is now toward the production of finer and finer rugs.

Today, the United States imports more rugs from India than from any other country, and most of these come from the northern province of Uttar Pradesh. Indian weaving is primarily a modified cottage industry, with most production coming from workshops located in small communities. The country's enormous population provides a ready source of inexpensive labor—in fact, at one time solid-colored rugs could be hand knotted in India for the same price that they could be made in other countries by machine. In addition, the fact that large numbers of people remain in the rural areas provides a degree of stability that's lacking in other countries, such as Iran, where the rug industry is losing workers to the rapidly industrializing urban centers.

Most of the weaving in India is done by men, who spend long hours in the workshops under the supervision of master weavers. All production is done under contract, and most of the materials are supplied from outside the weaving area. Once the rugs are completed, they're taken to the cities for cleaning, chemical washing, and shipping.

Since the Indian climate is hardly suited to the use of wool carpets, there's no domestic market for Oriental rugs. In other words, every carpet woven in India is, to all intents and purposes, intended for export. This means that changes to meet the demands of the market can occur very quickly. Not only do Indian rugs reflect current tastes in color and design, they're also being produced in finer and finer qualities. In many cases, it can be difficult to distinguish an Indian copy from the Iranian original; the softness of the wool is sometimes the only giveaway.

Practically every popular Persian carpet design is reproduced in India, although nomadic designs are less favored than finer workshop patterns. This is true not only because it's less profitable to copy coarser rugs, but also because these pieces come in smaller sizes, and Indian manufacturers are interested in meeting the market for larger rugs. This is also the case with Indian copies of Turkish, Caucasian, and Chinese patterns.

In general, Indian copies are worked in a greater variety of sizes than would be found in the original weaving areas. In fact, many designs are worked to scale all the way from mats to sizes suitable for very large rooms. This means that dealers are able to stock representative samples of these lines of rugs rather than the entire collection, thereby expanding their inventories and minimizing their investment at the same time. This also simplifies shopping for you, since you can quickly and easily look at the sample rugs as you're narrowing down your selection.

A Brief Tour of the Rug-Producing Countries

The names of Indian rugs are arbitrarily selected by the contractor or the importer; they have no geographical significance. It should be of no real concern to you—aside, perhaps, from satisfying your curiosity—whether a rug comes, say, from Agra or Jaipur. Most styles are patterned on the traditional designs listed in Chapter VIII, and one labeling practice that helps to eliminate confusion is the use of the prefix "Indo," followed by the traditional Persian, Turkish, or Caucasian name (PLATE LII). Unfortunately, this method of naming rugs isn't as prevalent as it ought to be.

When you look at a variety of Indian rugs, you'll find that pieces from different manufacturers and importers often have the same name or a similar design. To compare them you should use the same standards that you would in comparing Iranian rugs that come from the same district—the knot count, the quality of the wool, and the other factors described in Chapter V. Then compare the Indian copies with the Iranian originals.

There are also many trademarked brand names of Indian rugs on the market, which are usually presented by importers and manufacturers in catalogs of their "lines." These catalogs can be useful in comparative shopping, and they can also be valuable sources of information, but don't presume that any one of them is all-inclusive. New styles from different manufacturers appear on the market continually, and it's simply unrealistic to expect any one dealer to have a majority of the different styles that are available. However, the better shops will have a good representation of various lines and can help you narrow down your choices.

Although our main concern is with Indian pile rugs, it's impossible to ignore the very popular flat weave called a dhurrie that's also being imported from India in large quantities. Some dhurries are woven entirely of cotton, in a design of simple stripes, but they're also available in a great variety of simple geometrical designs. To determine the quality of dhurrie rugs, simply count the number of warps and the rows of wefts and compare them to the count in similar pieces that you're considering.

Another type of inexpensive Indian carpet is the numdah, a felted goat hair rug that's made in Kashmir. These soft rugs usually have either cream or black backgrounds, and are covered with designs of flowers and animals embroidered in wool.

In addition to the enormous number of styles that are produced, Indian rugs are also available in a wide range of qualities. Some of the simpler designs, inspired by Chinese rugs, can be duplicated with relatively few knots, while intricate, curving Persian designs are copied using up to three hundred knots per square inch (PLATE XXVI). In addition, standard-sized single- and occasionally double-wefted rugs are woven in Jaipur in Caucasian patterns, but with the feel (and the off-square knotting format) of Pakistani rugs.

The pile of Indian rugs is sometimes carved, or embossed, where different colors meet. This creates shadows that will give the rug more depth, and it's particularly useful in enhancing the appearance of rugs with relatively few knots per square inch, which would otherwise have a very flat look. However, better quality Indian rugs are usually woven according to the traditional technique, in which design elements are outlined with knots in a darker or contrasting color.

The overwhelming majority of Indian rugs are made with wool pile on cotton foundations. At one time, many of the cheaper rugs were woven on jute foundations, but this practice has become less common as the standards of the industry have been raised. In the same way, the use of cheaper, handspun wool, which sheds a great deal, has been supplanted by the use of the more desirable, but more expensive, machinespun wool. And as the reproduction of intricate Persian designs becomes finer and finer, silk rugs are also beginning to appear. In fact, the only drawback that remains in terms of the materials used in Indian rugs is caused by the government's rule that only domestic wool be used —when a blend of domestic and foreign wool would actually be preferable.

The rug industry on the Indian subcontinent has made great progress, and because of the social and economic upheavals in Iran, India seems likely to assume that country's role as the world's major producer of handwoven rugs. If you're interested in buying an Oriental rug solely for the way it looks, you may be able to save a good deal of money if you buy a rug from India or Pakistan. However, if investment is a factor in your decision, you'd be better off with a Persian rug. If your funds are limited, and you can be flexible about the size of the rug, it would probably be better to buy a smaller Persian rug than a larger rug, at the same price, from India or Pakistan. But before you make this kind of a decision, think carefully about what your priorities are. It's true that Indian rugs haven't had a good track record for resale, but how likely is it that you'll want to resell your rug? After all, aren't you buying an Oriental because you know it will last through so many years of use?

PAKISTAN

Pakistan shares India's weaving tradition, since both areas were united under the Mogul and later the British empires. However, when India and Pakistan were partitioned after the Second World War, their weaving industries took somewhat different courses. In Pakistan, the declining rug industry was revived with heavy government support that involved both subsidies and the introduction of modern methods of organization. Moslem weavers who had immigrated from India were joined by Turkoman weavers from the north in large weaving centers located in and around the cities of Lahore and Karachi. By the early 1960s, the Pakistani rug industry was booming, and since then hand-knotted carpets have been one of the country's leading exports.

Today, the Pakistani rug industry is organized around two methods of production. Many Pakistani weavers own their looms and enter into contracts with exporters, who in turn supply them with designs, materials, and sometimes cash advances. Rugs are also produced in large "factories" that come as close as possible to the mass production of Oriental rugs. In addition, the government has set up training programs for weaving teachers, and as a result, thousands of skilled weavers are added to the work force yearly.

At first, the revitalized Pakistani rug industry concentrated on reproducing the traditional Bokhara "elephant-foot" design—a choice dictated not only by the relative simplicity of the pattern, but also by the declining production of the original Bokharas in Russian Turkestan. Later, Caucasian designs were adopted, and now Persian rugs are also being copied.

Today, the Tekke Turkoman gul is the most widely used pattern in Pakistani Bokharas (PLATE XLIX). In addition to the traditional red background, Pakistani Bokharas are also being woven in a wide range of other colors, including rust, gold, orange, ivory, navy, and occasionally light blue or green, aqua, and tan. They're also available in a much wider range of sizes. The original tribal Bokharas are relatively small, but because of the simple repeating design format, Pakistani rug factories are able to produce Bokharas in many sizes and shapes, including runners. These range from 1 by 1 foot mats to 18 by 12 foot and even larger room-sized rugs. Some of the better-quality Pakistani Bokharas are programmed and are available in the entire range of sizes, while others, particularly lesser quality rugs, are only available in a few sizes.

An important feature of Pakistani Bokharas is the fact that they have more knots vertically than they do horizontally. This happens because the Pakistanis use a finer wefting than most other weaving areas and their yarn tends to be somewhat softer, so more rows of pile can be inserted. The usual knot counts per square inch of the better quality Pakistani Bokharas are 9/18 and 10/20 (the first number is the horizontal and the second the vertical).

The use of this knotting format can restrict the weaver's choice of designs because it's more suited to geometric shapes than it is to curving ones—and even geometric designs can still be somewhat distorted, particularly in the border patterns. This happens because the units of the designs aren't square. For example, when the cartoon of the end border is turned to form the side border a wide, squat design becomes a tall and narrow one.

Another design made in this rectangular knotting format is the Caucasian-influenced Kafkazi. These angularly patterned, thinly clipped rugs are made in the better range of qualities (knot counts from 10/20 to 12/24) in many colors other than the reds and blues of the original Caucasian rugs. Since Kafkazis are generally produced on speculation, they tend to be somewhat small; you won't find any that are larger than about 9 by 6 feet.

The most recent development in Pakistani weaving has been the reproduction of Persian designs. However, in order to produce the curving shapes featured in these patterns, Pakistani weaving had to be adapted to a square format so that roughly the same number of knots could be tied horizontally and vertically. This was accomplished by stacking one warp behind the other, a technique that allows more knots to be tied across the width of the rug and produces knot counts that range from 13/15 to 20/20.

Most Pakistani rugs in Persian designs are found in small sizes, from 7 by 4½ feet on down; larger sizes are available, but you'll pay a substantial premium for them. As is true of other Pakistani rugs, the colors don't necessarily follow the traditional Persian models—but rugs from Pakistani workrooms that are virtual duplicates of Persian classics have been appearing in greater and greater numbers on the international market.

Nevertheless, there's a wide range of qualities available in Pakistani versions of Persian patterns. When you're considering these rugs, it's best to avoid those that are coarsely executed because their designs tend to be somewhat blurry. In a case like this, you'd be better off with a blurry Persian rug—if only because its chances of increasing in value are probably greater.

No matter what their design or quality, Pakistani rugs are always woven with Persian knots on cotton warps; the lesser quality pieces are single wefted, and the rest are double wefted. In all cases, the wefting material is fine, and this permits the rows to be packed very close. Imported chrome dyes are used for the yarn, and since the native wools tend to be rather soft, the knotting is often worked in a blend of New Zealand and Belouch wool. Unfortunately, the pile of the coarser quality rugs could still do with some improvement.

When you're looking at rugs from Pakistan, a comparison of the knot counts is very important, but so too is an inspection of the surface of the carpet. Many Pakistani rugs have a comparatively high pile, and the rows of knots are often clipped irregularly during the weaving process. This happens because the knots are cut after several rows have been worked, rather than after every row, as is the case in other areas. This creates an indulating pile that may be impossible to correct. Of course, some unevenness can be acceptable, but you should compare a number of rugs to see just how much variation you can live with.

Despite these inconsistencies, the Pakistani rug industry seems to have an encouraging future, and the quality of its rugs is improving to fill the gap caused by declining production in Iran. However, although Pakistan has become a major source of rugs for the world market, most of the country's exports go to Europe. For this reason, the United States hasn't had much impact on the Pakistanis' choices of colors and styles, or on the programming of designs in a broad range of sizes.

Relatively speaking, rugs from Pakistan are good values at the moment, although their prices are steadily rising. As is the case with Indian rugs, if you're buying solely for looks, the odds are that you'll be able to find a Pakistani design that will be more reasonably priced than the original. For the time being, however, Pakistani rugs can't compete with those originals as far as investment is concerned.

CHINA

Pile rugs probably first arrived in China from Central Asia along the old silk trading route; the earliest examples that have survived have been dated to the seventeenth century, the end of the Ming dynasty. For the most part, Chinese rugmaking was limited to the colder regions in the north and northwest, and most carpets were produced for the court at Peking and the aristocracy.

In the nineteenth and early twentieth centuries, as European commercial and political interests in the country increased, the Chinese rug industry was subjected to more and more foreign influence. China's large population was a ready source of cheap labor, and, as in India, it was once possible to import plain-colored handmade goods from China that were cheaper than domestic machinemade goods. In addition, the Chinese could also weave rugs to order for a very reasonable price.

In the period between the two World Wars, China exported a large number of rugs that copied Persian, Turkish, Turkoman, and Caucasian designs. Chinese weavers also produced rugs in the Art Deco style that featured relatively large, colorful figures set on plain-colored fields, framed by simple borders in contrasting colors. However, with the advent of World War II and later the establishment of the People's Republic, this booming trade with the West declined. Today, the reestablishment of diplomatic relations with China and the relaxation of trade barriers have again opened the door to the importation of Chinese rugs.

Every phase of China's weaving industry is strictly regulated by the government, and its rugs are produced in government-run factories or workshops in Tientsin, Peking, Sinkiang, Shanghai, and a number of other weaving centers. Each of these centers operates independently in terms of its preferences in color and design, but since the government enforces very strict controls over the weaving itself there aren't any significant variations in quality from one area to another. Because of this standardization, the source of a particular Chinese rug isn't a matter that you need to be concerned about. In other words, you don't need to compare individual rugs that are woven to the same specifications because they'll all be the same quality.

Traditional Chinese carpets are immediately recognizable, even to someone with only a limited knowledge of rugs. Their colors—shades of blue, as well as ivory, gold, plum, rose, and tan —are quite different from the colors used in carpets in other areas of the world, and their designs are just as distinctive. Today, "traditional" Chinese rugs are still produced, but the Chinese palette has been expanded to include colors from other countries' weaving traditions, and some of the traditional Chinese designs have also been adapted to suit foreign tastes. In addition, ever-increasing numbers of designs from other countries are now being copied.

The most popular of the traditional designs is the classic Peking rug, which usually contains a circular medallion in an open field (PLATE XLVIII). The design elements are either familiar objects seen in nature (animals, flowers, or cloud patterns) or stylized

Chinese ideographs, usually framed by a simple, wide border.

Another group of traditional Chinese rugs consists of designs that show animals (dogs, pandas, or lions), mythic creatures (the dragon and phoenix), or stylized Buddhist, Taoist, and Confucian emblems (PLATE LX). Although these design elements have traditionally had symbolic meanings, today they're only used for their visual effect. They can be arranged symmetrically or asymmetrically, and sometimes the entire rug will show a scene.

The Chinese also weave rugs in the so-called "aesthetic" style, using a design based on the flowery images of the French Savonnerie and Aubusson rugs (PLATE XLI). These rugs tend to be more formal than the traditional Peking type, and they'll usually have a somewhat larger central medallion, also on an open field, with the surrounding designs formed by more complex multicolored floral arrangements.

Finally, the Chinese also produce "antique" rugs that are chemically washed to make them appear old (PLATE XLIII). These are made in traditional Chinese designs with backgrounds of ivory, rose, light blue, and gold, as well as in Persian designs and colors. These carpets are such good likenesses of the originals that in many cases it's difficult to distinguish between them. Not only are the colors and designs faithful, but even the feel of these pieces can be deceiving.

Most Chinese rugs are woven with wool pile, and all Chinese rugs use the Persian knot. Both warps and wefts are usually cotton, and both the yarn count and ply are set by government specifications. China also produces fine silk rugs, as well as carpets made of goat hair (PLATE XLIV). The latter are produced in the Peking style in a limited range of colors and are relatively reasonable in price. The materials for almost all rugs—whether wool, silk, or goat hair—are dyed with Chinese dyes.

The wool used in Chinese rugs may be either hand or machinespun. If you're unsure about which type has been used in any particular rug, just break open the pile and take a look at the strands. If the wool is machinespun, the yarn will be uniform in diameter from the base of the strand to the tip. If it isn't, you're probably looking at a rug woven from handspun yarn; these pieces should cost from ten to fifteen percent less than those with machinespun yarn.

China's rugs are usually woven with 5-ply yarns, in contrast to the 2-ply yarns used in Iran. Using thicker strands of yarn means that the carpets can't be as finely worked, but this is compensated for by the great regularity of the knotting and by leaving a somewhat deeper pile on the finished rug. The standard pile heights of Chinese carpets are 1/4, 3/8, 1/2, and 5/8 of an inch.

The density of the knotting in Chinese carpets is measured by the number of knots per linear foot, and this can vary from 70 to 240. The knot count is referred to as a "line"; in other words, a carpet with 70 knots per linear foot would be called a "70 line" carpet. Rugs woven in traditional patterns for the American market usually have a 5/8 inch pile, and are 90 line (90 knots to the foot). Persian designs have a 1/4 inch pile and are 120 line (because the designs are more intricate and require finer knotting); "antique" washed rugs usually have a 3/8 inch pile and range from 70 to 80 line; and silk rugs, which have a thinner pile, have up to 300 knots per linear foot.

The Chinese also have a method of weaving 70 to 90 line goods with what's called an "open back" technique. In this process, a heavier wefting is inserted between each row of knots. These white threads are clearly and unmistakably visible from the back of the carpet. Because carpets made with the open-back weaving technique have fewer rows of knots, they're also less dense. This means that they should cost about thirty percent less than the standard "closed back" rugs.

Another technique used in some Chinese rugs involves inserting pile through a canvas or duck backing with the aid of a hand-held tufting gun. When the rug is finished, a heavy cloth is glued to the back of the rug. These rugs are "handmade," but they are *not* handwoven. In fact, they don't even fit the definition of "Oriental rugs" and shouldn't really be sold as such.

In China, virtually all styles and qualities of rugs, except the Persian, are sculpted where different colors meet to produce depth and shading. Some Chinese rugs are chemically washed and then sculpted again before they're exported, a process that results in very deep shadings. Other rugs are washed after they arrive in the United States and aren't resculpted. This results in a more subtle contrast between adjoining colors, which will be reflected in a lower price.

Most Chinese rugs are available in standard sizes from 5 by 3 to 18 by 12 feet, and many designs are produced in a full range of sizes that can be matched almost exactly. These programmed lines are made under contract to exporters and are usually better quality rugs in all respects. The rest of the goods available from China are either contract merchandise that's been rejected for one reason or another or rugs that have been produced for the spot market. Export prices of all Chinese rugs are established by the government, and they're very competitive, particularly since China has been granted "most favored nation" trading status by the American government.

The general consensus among importers is that in the years to come China will be exporting a larger number of non-Chinese designs, as was the case during the period between the World Wars. However, the situation is somewhat different now, since the government has taken over the rug trade. Obviously, the crucial factors in the next few years will be the Chinese response to worldwide demand and the degree of cooperation that can be achieved between the governments of the United States and China and private American importers.

As far as investment is concerned, traditional Chinese patterns aren't likely prospects because their stylized patterns aren't in great demand. However, the Chinese use excellent materials, and their rugs often keep their fine appearance after a good deal of use. In this respect, Chinese versions of Persian designs can hold their value more securely than similarly designed rugs from India or Pakistan. The Chinese copies also tend to have a more classic look, and so they should have a more lasting appeal.

A Brief Tour of the Rug-Producing Countries

AFGHANISTAN

Afghanistan shares its western border with Iran, but the rugs produced in this country have more in common with the nomadic weaving of Central Asia than they do with the sophisticated Iranian carpets. Although there are some established weaving centers in the towns, most of the rugs that come from Afghanistan are still made by rural villagers and nomadic tribesmen. Unfortunately, the political turbulence of the region as well as the many internal problems that beset the country have disrupted the weavers' lives to such an extent that it's impossible to predict just what Afghanistan's rug production will be like in the future.

Afghanistan is still a very strict Moslem country, so the easiest way to begin identifying its rugs is to remember that designs from this area will hardly ever show animal or human forms. In addition, most rugs exported from Afghanistan are made in a few easily identifiable geometric styles and in dark, somber colors.

One of the most common, usually simply called the Afghan, or sometimes the Ersari, has rows of large, quartered octagonal guls (PLATES L, LVI). The field of the rug is usually a dark ruby red, and the guls, interspersed with stylized flowering branches, are woven in shades of blue and sometimes black, decorated with small accents of other colors, and surrounded by a geometric border. This arrangement forms the basic design of most Afghan-style rugs, although you can expect to see variations.

Afghan-style rugs are made in the weaving centers, as well as in the villages. The sizes range from 3 by 2 to 14 by 10 feet. Naturally, the village pieces tend to be somewhat smaller than the factory-made rugs, and their knot count tends to be lower. The knot count of factory-made Afghans can range as high as 150 knots per square inch, but usually it's much less. All Afghan rugs, whether from the factories or the villages, are made with native materials. Either chrome or natural dyes (or a combination of both) may be used.

You should be aware that some Afghan-style rugs are subjected to a process called gold washing in which the original red color is bleached out to shades of gold, coral, and amber that are quite different from the colors produced when the wool is dyed before it's woven. You can easily identify a rug that's been subjected to gold washing if you spread the pile from the face and expose the base of the knots, which won't have been reached by the bleach that was applied to the surface. The colors of these bleached Afghan rugs can be very pleasant and decorative, but there's some debate as to whether the process harms the pile fibers. The general consensus is that bleaching does involve at least the risk of damage.

Another major style currently exported from Afghanistan is the Belouch (PLATE LIX). Almost all Belouch rugs are made by nomads, and for this reason they're generally available only in small sizes—usually no larger than 5½ by 3 feet. Since the knotting is done on wool foundations using primitive horizontal looms, the finished rugs are relatively loosely woven. They're also quite reasonably priced.

Belouch designs are woven primarily in reds and dark blues, with white as an accent color, but you'll also see Belouchs that have been worked on a background of natural camel wool. The fields as well as the borders are composed of repeated geometric patterns.

Belouch weavers are particularly fond of prayer rugs, and their versions of this design can be distinguished by the fact that the niche, or mihrab, is rectangular rather than pointed, as it is in many other weaving areas. Another design that's commonly used is the familiar tree of life. There are also many distinctive tribal patterns, and in addition some Belouch designs also show a bit of Persian influence, which no doubt stems from the fact that many of these nomads have traditionally traveled to Iran to sell their rugs. In fact, you'll find that the Belouch rugs that are exported from Iran are of a somewhat finer quality than those shipped from Afghanistan. If you're interested in one of the latter, you should try to find the tightest weave that's available in the color and design you've chosen.

You may also run across at least two other types of rugs that are imported from Afghanistan. Dauvlatabad rugs often have lighter background shades than ordinary Afghan rugs, and they're almost always finer in quality. As a rule, Dauvlatabads are the most tightly woven rugs made in Afghanistan. However, they're usually found only in smaller sizes. The Mauri rugs that are also occasionally imported into the United States have a repeating gul design that's quite similar to the classic Tekke Bokhara pattern from Russian Turkestan. Mauri rugs usually have a comparatively high knot count, in excess of 150 knots per square inch.

Most rugs from Afghanistan continue to be moderately priced, despite the recent upheavals in the area, but how long this situation will last remains to be seen. Although rugs from this country may be interesting buys, their patterns are quite stylized, and the classic designs are limited in color and range. However, these rugs can be quite sturdy, and they often look very handsome in dens and offices, and with modern furniture. As far as investment is concerned, the more finely woven Belouch rugs appear to be the best buys for appreciation and resale.

ROMANIA

Romanian rug weaving can be traced back to the days when most of the Balkan peninsula was controlled by the Turkish empire. However, Romania's importance as a modern weaving center is due not only to its previous history, but also to the very effective organization of its ample labor supply. As in China, the central government has established strict standards of quality in the rug industry and has exerted controls on both color and design.

Virtually all Romanian weaving is made to order in government-established centers or cooperatives throughout the country. These large, modern factories are clean and well-lighted, providing working conditions that are generally much better than those in many of the other rug-producing countries. In these factories, the rugs are usually woven with Persian knots on aluminum looms. (This kind of loom has an advantage over the traditional wooden loom because it remains rigid, no matter how high the humidity might be—making it possible to weave rugs that have straighter, squarer dimensions.) Some weaving is also done in private homes, but this is usually contract labor by ex-factory workers who are supplied with materials and designs.

Romanian rugs are woven either on cotton or wool warps. The native wool is of very good quality—in fact, because of the similarity in the climate it's considered comparable to Iranian wool. There's also some blending of native wool with wool imported from New Zealand and Australia. German dyestuffs are used exclusively.

Romanian rugs are named for towns, rivers, and mountains, but these names have nothing to do with where the rugs are produced. Instead, they're used to classify the quality of the rugs in terms of knots per square meter. Several different qualities of rug may be manufactured in the same weaving center.

Although there may be subtle differences in the quality of wool from one district to another, it's safe to assume that all Romanian rugs with the same name are basically of the same quality. This means that once you've established your budget, you can concentrate on color and design. It's possible to find a Romanian version of almost every Persian style, as well as variations on these classic designs. Stylized geometric patterns that follow Caucasian designs are also produced, and in a wider range of sizes than the originals. However, both Persian and Caucasian designs are reproduced in typically Romanian colors.

Romanian rugs aren't quite as standardized as Indian rugs, and the designs aren't usually produced in a programmed range of sizes and colors. However, because of their fairly inflexible color schemes, it's possible to find a number of different designs in the same shades if you need to use several sizes of rugs in one room. The usual range is from 4 by 2 to 20 by 14 feet, including runners.

Romanian rugs have been criticized for the somewhat rigid look that results from their strictly supervised method of production, their limited color palette, and their literal adherence to the traditional models. However, in recent years, there's been constant improvement in all these areas, particularly in expanding the range of dyes to include colors that are more acceptable to American tastes.

In the past few years, imports from Romania have been grow-

Qualities of Rugs
Exported to the United States from Romania

	KNOTS *per sq. meter*	KNOTS *per sq. inch*
Cotton foundation		
Bucharesti	110,000	72
Brailu	160,000	105
Mures	200,000	130
Olt	250,000	165
Milcov	300,000	195
Wool foundation		
Transylvania	121,000	80
Brasov	160,000	105
Harmon	200,000	130
Postavaro	230,000	150
Mercerized cotton pile		
Moldova	200,000	130

ing as fast as those from Iran have been declining. Today, Romanian rugs are very competitively priced, particularly when they're compared with the Iranian goods on which they're modeled. Nevertheless, it's difficult to make an assessment of how well they'll hold their value because they haven't been exported for a long enough time to establish a performance record. However, by virtue of the fact that they're often copies of Iranian designs, it would seem sensible to assume, at least for the time being, that the originals are still a better investment.

THE SOVIET UNION

A number of areas in the Soviet Union have very old weaving traditions, but the two most important are the plains of Central Asia, where nomadic Turkoman tribes have roamed for over a thousand years, and the Caucasus Mountains, an inaccessible region between the Black and Caspian Seas that adjoins both Turkey and Iran. The Russians exerted some influence in both these areas for centuries, but actual government control, begun under the Tsars, wasn't consolidated until the Communist authorities took over. Today, with the establishment of the local Soviet republics, the nomadic population is gradually being resettled in villages and cooperatives, and the weaving of rugs is becoming much more standardized. Government factories in the Caucasus and Turkestan now produce large numbers of rugs for the domestic market, and also for export.

Before the Caucasus belonged to Russia, it was part of the Persian empire. But even while the region was under Persian rule, its weavers—isolated in mountain villages—maintained older traditions, using bright colors and strong geometric patterns, along with animal and human figures, rather than adopt the curving designs and garden imagery of Iran. Similar designs are still woven today, but in state-controlled factories located in the Republics of Armenia, Azerbaijan, Georgia, and Kazakstan (PLATE LV).

Modern Caucasian rugs are woven with the Turkish knot in a combination of basic pattern elements. These designs are much more standardized than the older Caucasian designs and, unlike their predecessors, they can't be identified with certain regions. These days, a rug may still be called a Kazak, a Shirvan, or a Derbent, but the name refers only to the pattern. Another significant change is the substitution of cotton for the warp and weft of the rugs—in older rugs, the foundation was almost always wool. Despite these changes, the modern Russian versions of traditional Caucasian rugs are generally quite well made, with extremely regular knotting and good quality wool. The range of sizes, which was traditionally fairly narrow, has remained so; almost all rugs from the Caucasus are under 9 by 6 feet.

Factories and workshops in the Central Asian republics of Turkmenistan and Uzbekistan also produce copies of older rugs, in this case the classic Turkoman designs known as Bokharas. These rugs, originally made by nomadic tribes, were named for the city that served as one of their central collection points. So-called Bokhara rugs are always a deep shade of red, with a repeating pattern of octagonal guls in dark blue, black, or brown, with white accents. The shape and color of the basic gul varied slightly from one tribe to another, and these differences were the traditional means of identifying the source of a particular rug. Today, many of the gul variations are interpreted in modern Bokharas and, as in the past, wool is used as the foundation material and the wool pile is tied with Persian knots. However, the modern factory-produced rugs are made in a greater range of sizes than the smaller nomadic Bokharas; they're now available in sizes up to 9 by 6 feet and larger.

Another less common type of rug that's produced in Soviet Central Asia is the Beshir (PLATE LVII). These rugs are unusual in that they're made in a variety of geometric designs rather than the repeated gul pattern that's usually seen in Turkoman rugs. Beshirs are very finely woven, and they have rather crowded fields that are often worked in stylized floral patterns. They're generally made in small room sizes and runners.

Rugs from the Russian Caucasus and Turkmenistan reproduce the older regional styles with a great deal of integrity and are made in very superior qualities. Most of these rugs are sent either to the domestic Soviet market or to European importers. They're exported to the United States only in limited quantities, primarily because they're subject to a prohibitive import duty. If you do run across some of these rugs, they'll be quite expensive, but you might still want to consider them, not only because of their greater investment potential but also because of their lovely designs and excellent weaving.

Spain

The Oriental rug probably came to Spain with the Moorish invaders, but once it arrived, the weaving process was adapted to include a technique that's still practiced today. Spanish weavers use a method in which knots are tied on every other single warp thread, with knot-bearing warps alternated in each row. This kind of knotting isn't found anywhere else in the world.

The styles of Spanish rugs that are sold in the United States are regulated mainly by importers, who usually specify classic Persian and Turkish designs in colors that are popular in this country. Many Spanish rugs are also woven with subtle color changes to simulate the look of older rugs (PLATE XIX). All of these carpets are woven with wool pile on cotton foundations.

Spanish rugs are made in a range of standard American sizes, as well as in custom sizes. However, they're available only in limited quantities and, because they're somewhat expensive, it seems likely that even fewer of them will be exported in the years to come. Despite their scarcity and their relatively high cost, Spanish rugs are more desirable for their appearance than they are for their investment potential.

TAIWAN

The rug industry in Taiwan was established by the Nationalist government following the Communist take-over of the mainland. As you might expect, rugs exported from Taiwan are almost always woven in classic Chinese patterns, particularly the Peking design (PLATE XLVI). In addition to the traditional colors, they're also available in a number of rich, deep backgrounds or in soft shades. Many designs and colors are programmed to be available in a wide range of standard sizes, and these rugs are generally of decent quality.

The Taiwanese are finding it difficult to maintain weaving centers in their steadily industrializing nation, despite the fact that weavers earn equal or better pay than factory workers. This situation, coupled with the normalization of American relations with the People's Republic, would seem to present the rug industry in Taiwan with an almost insurmountable challenge. And when you consider the construction, the quality of the wool, and the investment potential of Taiwanese rugs, you'll find that they deserve to be compared with Indian goods rather than with those from the mainland.

OTHER RUG-PRODUCING COUNTRIES

The countries mentioned so far certainly aren't the only ones that produce handwoven rugs. Although they're imported in limited quantities and sizes, you may run across hand-knotted rugs from a number of other areas. For example, Yugoslavia and Bulgaria, whose rug industries are organized much like that in Romania, produce lovely, well-constructed rugs, many of which are copies of Iranian designs. Rugs from Tibet are also appearing more and more frequently on the international market. These pieces are very much like those from China, but they tend to come in smaller sizes, and their colors, like those of the western Chinese provinces, are often somewhat brighter. Handwoven rugs are also exported from Egypt, Greece, Mexico, Morocco, Tunisia, and Poland—as well as a host of other minor rug-producing countries. However, the output from these areas is very small, and it's usually limited to flat-woven, kilim-style rugs.

CHAPTER VIII

A DIRECTORY OF
MAJOR RUG TYPES

 THERE'S NOTHING MORE BEWILDERING TO THE
first-time rug buyer than the variety of dif-
ferent names used to describe Oriental rugs.
And that's because there's an almost equally
bewildering number of systems by which
rugs are named. A rug can be named for the
style of its weaving (kilim, dhurrie), for its
general design (prayer rug, garden design), and for its size or use
(yastik, dozar, bag). It can be named for the people who made it
(Tekke, Kurd), the area from which those people migrated
(Belouch), or the period in which it was made (Shah Abbas). Most
often, though, an Oriental rug is named for the town, village, or
weaving area that it comes from.

Unfortunately, the process doesn't stop here, because these
geographical names are themselves applied in different ways. For
example, a rug can be named for the town in which it's sold
(Shiraz) or for the town in which it's actually manufactured (Kerman). And when the basic weaving area is very large—as is the
case of the country around Hamadan, in Iran, where rugs are
made in hundreds of villages—then the rugs are often named for
the individual village rather than the weaving area as a whole. In

addition, the selling or manufacturing of particular qualities and designs in particular places has given rise to still further variations —the names of some towns have been used to represent certain qualities of weaving (Ahar, Sarouk), as well as certain familiar designs (Shirvan).

As if all this weren't complicated enough, the spread of the weaving industry throughout the world has spawned still more ways of identifying rugs. In modern copies, the name of a traditional design is sometimes used with a prefix that indicates the country in which the rug was made (Indo-Kashan), but a rug can also be labeled simply by its country of origin. In some regions, such as Romania, the name of the rug (Bucharesti) refers only to the quality of the weaving and has no bearing on the design or the area in which the rug was made. Finally, when rugs are woven to order by importers and manufacturers, traditional designs and adaptations are often given new trademarks and brand names (Chindia) or described with adjectives (Princess, Royal) that are meant to imply a certain standard of quality.

Obviously, you can't master the complexities of identifying rugs your first (or even second) time out—but that doesn't mean you have to give up. If you've learned the basics of design and construction and you shop for your rug in the right place, you can use the directory that follows to make informed choices among various types and qualities of rugs.

In this directory, you'll find descriptions of well-known and long-established classifications—combinations of designs, colors, and weaving techniques—from the traditional rug-producing countries. As you might expect, many of these are Iranian. However, there are also entries for classic Turkish, Caucasian, Turkoman, and Chinese rugs. Each one was chosen not only because it's a distinctive and traditional rug type, but also because it's commonly found on the world market. Many of these rug types are also reproduced and adapted in a number of different weaving areas, but these copies (and any new names that might be used to describe them) are not given separate listings.

Each entry in the directory will give you the traditional source for a particular type of rug, as well as a general description of what the rugs are like in terms of color, design, and construction. You'll also be told what sizes are readily available in the original weaving area. If similar types of rugs are listed in the directory, these will be identified as cross-references. In addition, reproductions made in other countries will also be noted.

If you're confused about a rug name that you can't find in the directory, try looking in the index, in the glossary at the back of the book, or in the supplemental list at the end of the directory, which offers a brief rundown of rug types that are rarely or only occasionally found on the international market. If you still can't find the name, the chances are that it's a trademark or brand name that's been arbitrarily assigned by an importer or a dealer, and you'll have to ask more questions about it. If you find yourself in this situation, concentrate on gauging the quality of the rug, using the same criteria (outlined in Chapter V) that you would for any other rug.

The most important thing to remember when you're using the directory is that it should broaden your options rather than limit them. Start out by looking at colors and patterns in a very general way, and gradually weed them out until you find a style you like. Then explore the various sources that produce it and compare the qualities of rug that come from each area. If you've seen a rug that you like from India or Pakistan or China, instead of looking for that particular rug and that particular name, explore all the possibilities in the general category. There's a very good possibility that you can find other rugs that are just as attractive and functional as the one you originally had in mind. Your choice may be made clear by the difference in price, or you could find that a less expensive rug works better for you because it has a simpler design or a variation from the traditional colors that suits your needs. Just keep an open mind—and remember that no one dealer can stock every single type of rug that's made.

Above all, don't let the process of identifying a rug distract you from your basic goal—finding a rug that you like. Picking out an Oriental rug should be much more than an educational experience; it should also be an opportunity to simply enjoy the colors and patterns of all the beautiful carpets you'll be looking at. In the process, you're sure to find one that you'll want to enjoy in your own home.

Major Rug Types

Abadeh The weavers in this village in southwestern Iran produce carpets that have been influenced by much older Persian designs. The most common pattern, which resembles that made by the Qashqa'i weavers, is a geometrical one—a large diamond-shaped field filled with a medallion surrounded by small flowers and leaf patterns (PLATE VI). This design is tightly woven in short pile on fine cotton warps in bright, primary colors, particularly deep reds. Another design that appears less frequently is a repeating pattern of baskets of red flowers.

Abadeh rugs come in sizes ranging from 3 by 2 foot mats to 7-foot square carpets. They're moderate to expensive in price, and generally of good quality. SEE *Joshagan, Mei-Mei, Qashqa'i.*

The traditional Abadeh pattern is reproduced in decent quality Indian rugs that cost about half as much as the Iranian originals. These carpets are woven in the standard colors in sizes from 6 by 4 to 12 by 9 feet.

Afghan This type of rug, produced both by nomad weavers and in workshops, is one of the most widely imported rugs from Afghanistan. It is sometimes also called an Ersari Afghan. The design consists of large, squarish, quartered octagonal guls in deep blue, often with beige accents, repeated in columns and rows on a deep red- or gold-colored field (PLATES L and LVI). The borders will often feature a major stripe surrounded by many narrow guard stripes. These rugs have a very strong, masculine appearance.

The warps and wefts of Afghan rugs are almost always wool, and the only exception will be an occasional piece with a foundation made of goat hair. The quality of Afghan rugs can range from coarse to medium, with 25 to 75 knots per square inch; the finest come from Dauvlatabad. Afghan rugs are available in a wide range of sizes, from 3 by 2 to 14 by 10 feet. They're among the most modestly priced handmade rugs available, and they're good values. SEE *Belouch, Dauvlatabad.*

The relatively simple Afghan design is quite easy to copy—which is why you'll find "Afghans" that have been made in India, North Africa, and a number of other areas. Interestingly enough, Indian copies may be more finely knotted, and more expensive, than the originals on which they're modeled.

Afshar These geometrically patterned Iranian rugs are woven by seminomadic tribes. The majority have a short pile and are made in one basic size, about 6 by 5 feet, although somewhat larger sizes may appear from time to time. Quite a few saddle bags are also produced. The most common Afshar design is composed of one or more large diamond-shaped medallions on a field of stylized flowers (PLATE IX). Other patterns include stylized depictions of mosques or animals, and repeating patterns of either botehs or flowers.

Afshar rugs are worked on cotton or wool warps and wool wefts, primarily on a ground of bright red or blue, with white and yellow as the secondary colors. The quality of the wool varies, as does the general quality of the carpets, from coarse to medium. Afshars tend to be good buys among Iranian rugs, and the more finely woven ones are also good values. SEE *Shiraz.*

Ahar These are the most tightly woven rugs of the Iranian Herez family. The usual large medallion pattern can be slightly curving, and it's executed predominantly in shades of red and blue, with ivory accents. Ahar rugs have a medium pile height and are generally found only in smaller squarish sizes such as 4 by 3 feet, although some 10 by 8 and 12 by 9 foot rugs are made. These utilitarian rugs are also good investments since they're usually moderately priced. SEE *Herez, Mehriban.*

The traditional Ahar pattern is copied by Indian weavers.

Arak Although rugs from the Arak district of Iran (formerly called Sultanabad) are woven more coarsely, their designs are similar to those of rugs from the well-known neighboring town of

Sarouk. These designs come in a broad range of styles, from curving, lifelike plant and animal patterns to abstract, stylized geometrics, but they're usually executed on a brick-red field with a blue main border and accents of ivory, rose, yellow, and green. Sizes range from 10 by 8 to 18 by 12 feet.

Rugs from the Arak area can vary in quality (those of ordinary or poor quality are often called Mahals). Because of their low knot count, Arak rugs are among the least expensive carpets made in Iran. They can be good values, but only if you don't use them in areas where they'll get a lot of wear. SEE *Sarouk, Mahal.*

Ardebil Antique and semi-antique carpets from this region of northern Iran have little in common with the brightly colored, geometric rugs that are woven today in newly established weaving centers in the area. The modern designs, influenced by the Caucasian patterns made across the border in Russia, are usually composed of three large, connected diamonds worked in rows on an open field. Another common design features rows of octagonal lozenges on either an open or a well-covered ground; a third is made up of a single geometric medallion on a well-covered field (PLATE XXIX). The predominant colors are usually deep blue, ivory, yellow-green, or bright red, although earth tones are also being introduced.

Ardebil rugs are worked on cotton warps with fully stacked Turkish knots, and the pile height is kept relatively short. These rugs range in size from 3 by 2 to 14 by 10 feet and larger; many sizes of runners are also produced. Ardebil rugs differ from Caucasian rugs in that their wool isn't as lustrous, their pile is higher, and they're available in larger sizes. The quality of an Ardebil rug is generally described as coarse to medium, twenty to thirty percent finer than its counterpart, the Meshkin—and proportionately more expensive. SEE *Meshkin, Shirvan.*

As Iranian rugs become harder and harder to find, even the more moderately priced styles are beginning to be reproduced in India. Indian versions of Ardebil carpets are worked in the typical higher pile of Indian rugs, and are fairly similar in color to the originals. They're available in sizes from 6 by 4 to 14 by 10 feet.

Bakhtiari   These dark and richly colored rugs are made by nomads and villagers in southern Iran. The most prevalent design consists of a series of ellipse-shaped medallions filled with floral patterns and set against an extremely well-covered field. Another common Bakhtiari pattern is a garden design made up of a series of connected diamond- or square-shaped compartments containing floral or animal figures (PLATE XXXIV). The tree of life pattern is also popular. The colors used in all these designs are deep, bright, and strong; red and blue are usually the predominant shades, with yellow, brown, green, and white accents.

Bakhtiari rugs are normally woven with Turkish knots on cotton foundations, and the wefts are somewhat loosely packed— they're often very easy to spot from the back of the rug. The pile is of medium height, and the weave can vary from coarse to medium. Bakhtiari rugs are made in sizes that range from 6 by 4 to 10 by 7 feet, although larger, square rugs are also fairly common.

The best quality rug from the Bakhtiari region is called Bibi- baff. In addition, you may also run across Bakhtiaris that have been named for the specific remote village where they're woven. This practice is common in many areas of Iran, and a good rug dealer will be able to explain any local names that might be un- familiar to you.

Basmakci   This Turkish weaving district is becoming increasing- ly important in the country's rug industry. Basmakci produces tra- ditional Turkish designs—Bergama, Ghiordes, Oushak, and others—as well as copies of Caucasian styles. Even though none of these patterns are original to Basmakci weavers, they're still able to produce rugs with a much fresher, more distinctive look than many other rugs that copy traditional designs (SEE *cover photo- graph*). These rugs are woven in strong colors on woolen warps.

Basmakci rugs are made in sizes that range from small mats to 14 by 10 foot carpets, as well as runners. They're moderately priced, and since they're usually made in the smaller sizes they don't tend to be terribly expensive.

Belouch (Baluchi)   Many of the Belouch tribes are still nomads, and they roam throughout eastern Iran, western Pakistan, and

Afghanistan. Iranian Belouch rugs are woven in and around the city of Meshed in the northeastern part of the country, and Meshed serves as their collection center. The designs of these rugs are always geometric (PLATE LVIII), and the most common are the tree of life pattern, the prayer rug, and the classic Bokhara pattern of columns of octagonal guls. All these designs are worked in dark shades of red, blue, and brown, with camel and ivory accents. In fact, somber colors are one easy way to recognize Belouch rugs.

Iranian Belouchs are worked in Persian knots on cotton warps, and are usually hard wearing. Their quality can range from coarse to medium; the best will have up to 100 knots per square inch. Iranian Belouchs are usually no larger than about 6 by 4 feet.

Belouch rugs made in Afghanistan are often collected in the city of Herat. These rugs are woven on wool foundations in traditional designs similar to those found in Iranian Belouchs (PLATE LIX). Generally, they're more closely woven than their Iranian counterparts, with a shorter pile. They too are normally made in small sizes, although coarsely woven larger carpets do appear on occasion. SEE *Afghan, Bokhara.*

Beshir   This style of rug was once woven by Turkoman tribes in central Asia, and is now produced in Russian Turkmenistan and Afghanistan. Beshir rugs are unusual in that they're produced in a variety of geometric designs rather than the repeated gul pattern that's usually seen in Turkoman rugs. These designs are usually very crowded, and they often include floral patterns (including the classic Herati motif) or cloud bands. The borders are formed by many narrow bands in alternating colors.

Beshir rugs are usually worked on a field of dark blue, with the design itself in shades of red with distinctive yellow accents (PLATE LVII). Beshirs are finely woven on wool warps with a medium pile height. They come in small room sizes and in runners. Beshirs are perhaps the finest quality Russian rugs imported into America, and this, coupled with the high tariffs imposed on Russian goods, means that they're quite expensive.

Bibicabad   These rugs are produced in the country around Hamadan in western Iran. They can easily be identified by their pattern—a repeated red, blue, and white Herati fish design, with or without a central medallion. The weaving is of coarse to medium quality, done on cotton warps. Unfortunately, the single weft and the higher pile of these rugs tend to obscure and "fuzz" their patterns, so it's wise to consider only the better quality rugs from this area. Bibicabads are made in room sizes, and occasionally in long runners. Although they're now in somewhat short supply, Bibicabads are still among the more moderately priced Iranian rugs. SEE *Hamadan.*

Bidjar   This is the so-called "iron rug" of Persia—a stiff, heavy carpet that's quite thick and dense. Bidjar carpets were once woven on wool foundations, but they're now worked on cotton warps and wefts, using the finest Kurdish wool for the pile. Each knot is fully stacked, since the warps are set at two levels, one on top of the other. When each row is completed, a metal rod or a heavy metal comb is inserted and hammered upon to pack down the triple wefts. These extremely durable, medium-pile rugs are produced in rich, dark colors—primarily reds and blues—usually in the Herati design with French-style roses in the borders and corners (PLATE XIV).

Bidjars are also woven in the Minahani pattern, as well as in a design that features a large medallion anchored with palmettes, placed on either an open or a well-covered field. Bidjar rugs are available in a full range of sizes, from mats to 12 by 9 foot carpets. They're very expensive, but well worth the cost because they're so durable. They also make very good investments. SEE *Kurd.*

Bokhara   The city of Bokhara was once an important trade center in Turkestan, and in the past all rugs sent there for resale were simply called Bokhara rugs. Today our means of classifying rugs are much more precise, so when we talk about modern Bokhara rugs we're referring to a general type of Turkoman rug that's woven in northeastern Iran and in Russia.

Bokhara rugs are worked in the classic Turkoman "elephant's foot" octagon, also known as a gul. This pattern is repeated in rows and columns, usually on a deep red field (PLATE LI). Traditionally, each nomadic group had its own distinctive variation of the gul, and many are still reproduced in modern Bokharas. The most famous are the Tekke, the Yomut, and the Salor.

Bokhara rugs are woven on woolen foundations, with excellent quality wool, and the pile is clipped short. Unfortunately, very few of these rugs are imported into the United States from Russia, in part because of the high tariffs. When they do appear, they're usually only available in sizes up to 9 by 6 feet. Iranian Bokharas are available in sizes that range from 3 by 2 to 10 by 7 feet. SEE *Afghan, Beshir, Belouch.*

The relatively simple and adaptable Bokhara pattern was the first to be produced in Pakistan. There and in India it's made in a vast range of sizes, from 1 foot square mats up to 18 by 12 foot and larger room sizes. In addition to the traditional red color scheme, Pakistani and Indian Bokharas are found in rust, tan, orange, light and dark blue, green, aqua, and gold (PLATE XLIX). The pile height is high, and the wool is soft. Unlike the Russian and Iranian Bokharas, the Indian and Pakistani versions are woven on cotton warps and wefts. When you're looking at these rugs, it's wise to keep in mind the fact that they can vary a great deal in quality, from very poor to very fine—so it's crucial to make a comparison between the knot counts of a number of pieces in addition to inspecting the evenness of the shearing. Also make sure that the design elements are uniform in size and shape throughout the carpet. Look at the pattern in several different places and make sure the designs match.

Borchalou (Bordchelu)   These rugs from the Hamadan region of Iran feature a brightly colored medallion on a well-covered field which is often decorated with the Herati pattern. The field is in red or white; the designs in red, blue, gold, and green.

Borchalous are made with medium-quality wool, and the pile is high. Like almost all the rugs from the Hamadan area, these carpets are single-wefted. Borchalous are becoming harder and harder to find, and they're only available in 5 by 3½ and 7 by 5 foot dimensions, as well as in the long, narrow kellegi size that's usually two or three times longer than it is wide. All Borchalou rugs fall in the medium price range. SEE *Hamadan.*

Dauvlatabad   This heavy-duty carpet is made in northern Afghanistan. Dauvlatabads are woven with wool pile on wool foundations in conventional Bokhara patterns. The field color is either red or gold, and the designs are worked in dark blue and black. After the weaving has been completed, some of the red rugs are stripped to gold tones through a bleaching process known as gold washing.

Dauvlatabads are made in a range of metric sizes geared to the European market. The largest are usually about 13 by 10 feet. They're still fairly moderate in price, although they cost about fifty percent more than regular Afghan carpets. In general, Dauvlatabads are the best quality rugs made in Afghanistan. SEE *Afghan, Bokhara.*

Dergezine (Dargazine)   This well-defined and brightly colored rug from the Hamadan district of Iran features either a detached floral design or a repeating pattern that fully covers a red or white field (PLATE XXII). The most common design elements seen in Dergezines are the Herati and the Seraband, with or without a central medallion.

Dergezine rugs are woven in medium-quality wool using a single weft, and they're produced in sizes ranging from tiny mats to 12 by 9 foot carpets, as well as in runners. Dergezines are fairly coarse in quality. Although they were once among the least expensive rugs made in Iran, they've now risen into the moderate price range. SEE *Hamadan, Injelas, Kabutarahang.*

Dosemealti   These village rugs from western Turkey are woven on woolen foundations, often in an unusual dark green color, as well as in the more traditional red, indigo, and ivory. Dosemealti patterns feature strong geometrics, usually incorporating a double prayer arch with a column of three diamond medallions. These designs bear some resemblance to the Kazak patterns that come from the Caucasus, except that they're made in a greater variety of colors. Dosemealti rugs are available in sizes that range up to 9 by 6 feet, as well as in narrow runners. SEE *Milâs, Kazak.*

A Directory of Major Rug Types

Gabeh   These rugs from southern Iran are woven with undyed wool in shades of brown, grey, black, and off-white. The pile is left quite long. As you might expect, Gabeh patterns are very simple and uncluttered, with many open spaces. Since Gabehs are coarsely woven, they tend to be among the most inexpensive rugs made in Iran. They're available in a range of sizes up to about 10 by 7 feet.

Hamadan   The city of Hamadan is the center of a large weaving area in western Iran that encompasses hundreds of villages and tens of thousands of looms. Each village in the Hamadan district has its own distinctive weaving tradition, and these dictate the precise patterns that are used and the sizes that are made. However, almost all rugs from the Hamadan region use the same basic color palette: the designs are woven in primary colors, usually with backgrounds of ivory, red, blue, or brown.

Hamadan designs are generally fairly simple, and they usually incorporate floral elements. You may have heard of one of the most famous of these patterns, which was named for the village of Herat. At one time, rugs worked in the Herati pattern were exported from Hamadan in large numbers, but since the Second World War fewer and fewer of them have been produced.

Rugs from the Hamadan region are woven with Turkish knots on cotton foundations and, except for those called Kasvins, they all have single wefts. This produces a distinctive herringbone pattern on the back of the carpet. Camel hair is often used for the pile, and when wool is used it ranges from coarse to medium in quality. The pile is usually sheared to a medium height. Although the dimensions of the rugs vary from village to village, most Hamadan carpets are made in comparatively smaller sizes, from mats to 12 by 9 foot room sizes; the area also produces many runners.

Rugs from the Hamadan district are at the lower end of the price scale of Iranian rugs; the cheapest are often called Mosuls. Unfortunately, you'll find that in these carpets the lower knot count often obscures the pattern. SEE *Bibicabad, Borchalou, Dergezine, Injelas, Kabutarahang, Kasvin, Mazlaghan.*

Hereke The area in and around this city in western Turkey shares a common design heritage with the Iranian city of Tabriz, so you'll find that there are still many similarities between their patterns, which are generally very intricately drawn, with repeating and intertwining floral elements (PLATE X) and rich, deep colors. In addition to the traditional patterns, Hereke rugs are also found in the classic Ottoman prayer designs.

Hereke is famous for both its silk and wool rugs. The silk pieces are woven in shades of red, blue, and ivory, and the knotting is extremely dense, averaging about 720 knots per square inch. These rugs are made in sizes up to 6 by 4 feet, and many of them are produced in a flat weave with accents in gilded thread. Some artificial gold is also used.

Woolen Hereke rugs are made in sizes that range from 9 by 6 to 12 by 9 feet, primarily in an area along the Black Sea. These rugs are also produced in fine qualities, with either 240 or 420 knots per square inch. In fact, Hereke rugs, whether silk or wool, are among the finest rugs woven today—and they command prices to match their quality.

Herez Rugs from the city of Herez in northwestern Iran are produced in the classic medallion and corner design, a somewhat large-scale, angular pattern that's copied in dozens of nearby villages (PLATE XXXIII). Rugs from this area are usually woven in brick or rust reds, and occasionally in deep blues.

Herez rugs are produced in a range of sizes that begins at about 5 by 3 feet; it's quite rare to find any sizes smaller than this. There can be quite a great deal of variation in the quality of the wool and the skill of the weaving, so it's important to make a careful comparison between a number of rugs from this region before you make a final selection. (The most coarsely woven rugs from the area are sometimes called Gorevans because that town once produced many poor quality rugs.) In general, Herez carpets are among the medium-priced Iranian rugs. SEE *Ahar, Mehriban, Karaje, Serab.*

The popular Herez pattern is made in India both in the bright, deep, traditional colors and also in softer earth tones. These are produced in standard sizes from 6 by 4 to 14 by 10 feet, and occasionally even larger. When you're looking at these rugs, you'll often hear them described as Serapi carpets, a name that's incorrectly applied to certain older pieces from Herez, particularly those with designs that feature larger solid-colored areas and less detail. Indo-Serapis will be woven in the same style.

Injelas (Ingeles) Rugs from the village of Injelas in the Hamadan region of western Iran are usually woven in Herati, Seraband, and detached floral designs (PLATE XXI) in bright colors against a red field. The main border is generally a deep blue. Like most other rugs from the Hamadan region, Injelas rugs are woven with a single weft, and the pile height is medium to high. These rugs are available in mat and throw rug sizes, as well as in runners. Injelas carpets are among the more reasonable priced Iranian rugs. They're generally rated as fair to medium in quality. SEE *Hamadan, Dergezine.*

Isfahan (Isphahan) The old capital of the Safavid dynasty is still an important craft center and produces some of the finest rugs made in Iran. The designs used in Isfahan are inspired by the elegant and intricate patterns that were first produced by the court weavers of the sixteenth and seventeenth centuries. They usually consist of intertwining arabesqued vines, flowerheads, and palmettes surrounding a central medallion, with corner designs that are adapted from the medallion (PLATE III). Another popular style made in Isfahan is the picture rug, particularly illustrations of scenes from the works of Omar Khayyam. All these designs are usually worked in a wide range of light, bright contrasting colors, without the subtle gradations seen in older Iranian weaving.

When you're looking at Isfahan rugs, it's important to avoid one possible source of confusion—some modern rugs that are called Isfahans are actually made in the area around Meshed. These rugs bear no resemblance to the rugs actually made in Isfahan; there are great differences between the two areas not only in the colors used, but also in the quality of the materials and in the weaving.

157

Isfahan rugs generally have cotton foundations and a closely woven wool pile; silk is often used as a pile accent. The finest rugs from Isfahan are woven on silk warps with wool pile and have over 650 knots per square inch. All Isfahan rugs are available in a range of sizes, from mats to room-sized carpets that are 14 by 10 feet and up. The larger carpets can be less finely woven, but if they are finely woven, they'll be very expensive.

History has shown that the best quality product appreciates at the fastest rate. For this reason, rugs from Isfahan, although expensive, are wise choices for buyers who are interested in the investment value of a rug. In fact, fine Isfahans have such a sure value that they can almost be used as currency. Small pieces are easy to store or display, and they're often used as wall hangings. SEE *Nain, Kashan, Qum.*

Isfahan patterns are copied in "European" colors by Romanian weavers.

Isparta (Sparta)   This old Turkish weaving region produces rather coarse rugs that are woven on cotton warps in pastel or earth tones. The designs are copies of Persian and sometimes Chinese originals, in a wide range of sizes. Copies of Kerman designs are particularly common; these look very much like the Indo-Kerman copies, except that they aren't sculpted.

Rugs from Isparta have a medium to high pile and a comparatively low knot count. Since they're made on contract and earmarked for the European market, not very many ever find their way to America.

Joshagan   Rugs from Joshagan are the exception to the generalization that geometric designs are only found in coarse weaving. These fine pieces from central Iran have a diamond-shaped medallion on a very well-covered field of stylized, geometrical flowers and stepped spandrels (PLATE VII). Their primary colors are red and blue.

Joshagans are worked in Persian knots on cotton warps and wefts, with a low to medium pile. They're usually found in sizes tailored to the European market; 10 by 7 and 12 by 8 feet are the most common.

Joshagan rugs are expensive, but their high knot count (which can range up to 160 per square inch) also makes them good values. For investors, it's worthwhile to note that the supply of Joshagans is becoming relatively small. Since the quality of the weaving can vary from medium to good, it's important to compare a number of pieces before you make a final choice. The best quality Joshagans are called Mei-Mei. SEE *Abadeh, Mei-Mei.*

The Joshagan design, slightly expanded, is reproduced in rugs from Romania, using somewhat softer nontraditional colors, as well as earth tones. Joshagan designs are also occasionally copied in India.

Jozan This village lies halfway between the Arak and Hamadan weaving districts in Iran. Its rugs are traded in Hamadan even though they bear a closer resemblance to the Sarouk rugs that come from Arak. In fact, the word "Jozan" is sometimes used as a prefix to describe some Sarouks (PLATE IV). One way to tell the difference is that Jozans are woven on cotton warps using plain-colored wefts, while Sarouks are woven with blue wefts.

Jozan carpets are thick and heavy, they're woven with the best quality wool, and the pile is of medium height. Rich primary colors predominate, and the most common design is a medallion with either a Shah Abbas or Herati pattern in the field. Sizes range from 3 by 2 foot mats to 14 by 10 foot carpets. Jozans are very expensive, but they're also very well made—and they've proven to be sound investments. You'll rarely find a poor piece from this area. SEE *Sarouk, Melayer.*

Jozan carpets are reproduced by Indian weavers.

Kabutarahang These single-wefted rugs from the Hamadan district of Iran have a medium to high pile and are usually woven with blue, ivory, and sometimes green designs on a bright, cardinal-red field. Another popular color scheme features dark blue patterns worked on a white background. Detached floral and Herati designs are commonly used, as are the Seraband and other Sarouk patterns. In addition, medallion designs with both open and well-covered fields are also produced.

Kabutarahang rugs are available in room sizes that range from 9 by 6 feet to 18 by 12 feet. They're among the low to moderately priced Iranian rugs. SEE *Hamadan.*

Karaje (Karaja) The village of Karaje is in northwestern Iran, near the Russian border. The distinctive design of its rugs—a repeating pattern of large, lozenge-shaped medallions surrounded by narrow borders—is similar to the design of rugs from neighboring Herez, and both show the influence of the Caucasian weaving tradition (PLATE VIII). Unfortunately, Karaje rugs are woven with a single weft that isn't always beaten down well. The wool used for the pile is thick, and so the knot count is comparatively low.

Rugs from Karaje are available in earthy tones of brick and blue, and in two different shades of ivory. Their sizes range from 3 by 2 foot mats to 12 by 9 foot room-sized carpets. Some runners are also produced, usually in smaller sizes. Karajes are in the low-to medium-price range among Iranian rugs. Because of the variations in the quality of the weaving, it's especially important to make a careful comparison of several pieces when you're considering these rugs. SEE *Herez.*

Karaje designs are copied by Indian weavers.

Kashan (Keshan) The Kashan is one of the most expensive wool-pile rugs made in Iran. These fine carpets are commonly woven in the Shah Abbas pattern, with or without medallions or corner pieces (PLATE V). Picture rugs and variations on a classic vase medallion are also produced, as well as some geometric designs featuring very stylized repeated elements that look like snowflakes. Many modern Kashans are worked in as few as five colors and have a predominantly blue appearance. In addition, Kashans are also still woven in the classic deep blue and burgundy field colors.

Kashan rugs are woven on cotton foundations in Persian knots with either silk or wool pile. The wool is of excellent quality, and can be very silky. In addition, the knots are quite firmly packed to form a dense, stiff carpet, the quality of which is determined by the size of the weft threads. The standard sizes for

Kashans are 4 by 2, 5 by 3, 6 by 4, 12 by 9, and 13 by 10 feet.

As is the case with all Iranian carpets, the qualities of Kashans can vary greatly. You should also be aware that some so-called Kashans, particularly those available in larger sizes, are actually made in Yezd, and that these tend to be of lower quality. Since the designs are so similar, the name is much less important than the knot count when you're comparing rugs from these two areas. Both Kashans and Yezds are expensive; the very finest are among the most costly Iranian wool pile rugs. Both types have proven to be good investments. SEE *Yezd, Isfahan, Nain, Qum.*

The Kashan style has been reproduced in India in a variety of sizes and colors, and at a reasonable cost (PLATE xx). As the years go by, more and more Indo-Kashans are being seen in the classic red and blue style; in fact, the Indian weavers generally seem to be making much closer copies than they have in the past. Pakistani Kashans tend to be both finer and costlier than those made in India, and they're also usually produced only in smaller sizes. They're surprisingly high priced, as are the more finely woven pieces from India.

Kasvin (Kazvin) The stout, double-wefted Kasvin rugs are produced in the Hamadan district of western Iran, but they bear no resemblance to the rugs woven in the hundreds of other villages near that city. Kasvin rugs are worked primarily in red, blue, ivory, and green on medium-to-fine cotton warps and wefts with a high and dense pile. The designs resemble those of the open-field Kerman, the detached floral Sarouk, or the intricately patterned Kashan. In fact, Kasvins can be described as domestic copies of these other Iranian designs.

Unfortunately, Kasvin rugs are now being produced in smaller and smaller numbers. When they are available, they're among the medium-priced Iranian rugs. Kasvins are made in a full range of sizes, from mats to larger room sizes. SEE *Kerman.*

Kayseri (Keyseri) These short-pile rugs are woven in villages between the towns of Kayseri and Sivas in eastern Turkey. The area produces a very broad range of designs, from sophisticated, curving Tabriz and Isfahan patterns that have been influenced by the tastes of local Armenian weavers (PLATE XI) to much more geometric styles. The traditional prayer rug is also popular in the region. All these patterns are worked in the red, blue, or ivory grounds that are favored in the European market.

The workmanship of Kayseri rugs is generally very good, which isn't surprising in view of the fact that large numbers of Armenian weavers have remained in the area. All Kayseris have cotton foundations. Some have a very finely woven silk pile, with up to 400 knots per square inch. Others are woven with a mercerized cotton pile that resembles silk; these have up to 165 knots per square inch. Kayseris are produced in sizes that range from small mats to 14 by 10 foot carpets. All are moderate or slightly higher in price.

Kazak   The name Kazak is given to rugs from the Transcaucasian Soviet Republics that feature large, relatively simple, geometric designs in sharply contrasting colors, usually bright reds, greens, and yellows (PLATE LV). Kazak rugs often include primitive snake-like patterns, cloud bands, and crests. The pile is relatively thick, and it's now often worked on cotton foundations rather than the traditional wool. Kazaks are good medium-quality rugs. Unfortunately, they're being made in smaller and smaller quantities, and even when they are available, the largest size is generally about 8 by 5 feet.

Copies of the classic Kazak pattern are now being woven in Turkey, particularly in Dosemealti, and in Romania (PLATE LIV). Other adaptations in nontraditional colors are made in India and Pakistan in a wide range of sizes, including runners. Interestingly enough, many of these copies are finer than the originals, and most have a shorter pile.

Kerman (Kirman)   The Kerman district of southeastern Iran is a bleak and desolate area, hardly the sort of place where you'd expect to find some of the most sophisticated and expensive rugs in the world. The Kerman patterns have been influenced by the flowery French Aubusson rugs; their pastel colors are almost always displayed on an open field of champagne, light or dark blue, dusty rose, or light green (PLATE XLII). These pieces are woven with finely spun pile and foundation yarns, and with triple wefts. They're left with a high pile. Unfortunately, the pile height sometimes tends to obscure the definition of the rug's design, a situation that's further complicated when the rug is chemically washed. Tradititional high-pile Kermans are available in perhaps the widest range of qualities found in Iran. For this reason, their knot count is an especially important consideration.

Shorter-pile Kerman rugs are also beginning to appear on the American market, in a more limited range of sizes than the traditional higher pile Kermans, which are available in as broad a range of sizes as any Iranian rugs. The new shorter-pile Kermans have intricate, scrolling designs in brighter colors, and they're reminiscent of an older period of Iranian weaving. These rugs tend to be even more costly than their already expensive predecessors. SEE *Kasvin, Yezd.*

The Aubusson-inspired Kerman design has been a staple of the Indian rug industry. However, unlike the originals, Indian Kermans are sculpted where the colors meet to compensate for their much lower knot count (PLATE XLV). There are many, many variations of this basic style produced in India, as well as in China (PLATE XLI) and the Balkans.

Konia (Konya/Ladik) These medium-pile rugs are made in southern Turkey around the town of Ladik, just to the north of the old capital of the Seljuk Turks, Konia. They have the same feeling as the dense, heavy Persian Bidjar rugs, but they're woven in floral patterns reminiscent of the designs used in Kashan and Tabriz (PLATE XXXIX). Many prayer rugs are also produced, and these usually incorporate the stylized tulip that's popular among the region's weavers.

Ladik and Konia carpets are worked in wool pile on cotton foundations, usually with about 160 knots per square inch. The sizes range from 6 by 4 to 12 by 9 feet. Rugs from this area, which were once moderately priced, are becoming more and more expensive. SEE *Kashan.*

Kula Some woolen-warped rugs in traditional Kula and Ghiordes prayer designs are still woven in the area near this city in western Turkey (PLATE XXXVII), but for the most part the patterns now made in Kula follow the tastes of the European market. These are usually stylized floral designs, although a pattern that features a geometrical medallion with an open field is also popular. All Kulas are worked in pastel colors.

Most Kula rugs have a medium pile height and are of fair to medium quality. They're made in sizes that range from small mats to 10 by 7 foot carpets, and they're usually moderately priced.

Many traditional Kula designs are now produced in Romania.

Kurd At one time, nomadic Kurdish tribesmen roamed throughout the Middle East, but today many Kurds have settled in northern Iran, and most Kurdish rugs now come from this region. These colorful rugs are somewhat coarsely woven on wool warps and wefts, and a large number of them are flat-woven. Although most of the designs used by Kurdish weavers are geometric, there are no uniquely Kurdish patterns.

Kurdish rugs are usually no larger than 7 by 4 feet in size. They're among the more moderately priced Iranian rugs. SEE *Bidjar, Senneh.*

Mahal These double-wefted, coarsely woven rugs are produced in the Arak district of Iran. Mahal weavers have no distinctive traditional patterns, so they take their designs from other areas. The most common is a large-scale, all-over, floral pattern or a medallion, but repeating patterns (such as the Herati) are also used. The border is usually a simple one made up of three bands.

Mahal rugs are woven in interesting shades of red and blue, with rather coarse knotting. The finished rugs are quite soft and supple. They're available in sizes from 12 by 9 to 18 by 12 feet. Mahals are moderately priced in comparison with most other Iranian rugs. SEE *Arak, Sarouk.*

Mazlaghan The pattern woven in this village in the Hamadan district of Iran is quite easy to identify—the elongated field is usually worked in red, and the large medallion is anchored with dark blue spandrels. In addition, the end borders are very narrow, and the entire field is outlined with a pattern that looks like a zig-zag thunderbolt.

Mazlaghans are only made in small sizes, since their patterns would be overwhelming in larger rugs. They're generally of medium quality, and are among the medium-priced Iranian rugs. SEE *Hamadan*.

Mehriban (Mehrivan) There are two villages in Iran called Mehriban, and each produces a different type of rug. Those that come from the village in the Herez district are woven with some-what coarse wool on cotton foundations in typical Herez designs and colors. These rugs are made in medium room sizes and are of fair to medium quality. SEE *Herez*.

The Mehriban rugs that come from the Hamadan weaving district are worked in floral patterns and are available in smaller sizes. SEE *Hamadan*.

Mei-Mei Rugs from this town in central Iran are quite similar to those made in neighboring Joshagan, but they're of finer quality and are more expensive. SEE *Joshagan, Abadeh*.

Melayar (Malayer) Rugs from this minor Iranian weaving center, located between the Arak and Hamadan districts, bear a great resemblance to those from Sarouk. However, Melayar rugs can be distinguished by their scrolling vine borders and their somewhat rectangular, well-covered medallion fields. The most common colors used in these rugs are reddish orange, deep blue, and beige.

Melayar rugs are made with very fine wool in sizes from mats up to about 7 by 4 feet. They're generally less expensive than rugs produced in Sarouk. SEE *Sarouk*.

Meshed (Mashad) Rugs from the Meshed district in northeast-ern Iran usually have a round floral medallion on a bluish red, semi-covered field, which is often worked in the Herati pattern. Meshed rugs are woven on cotton foundations, and the dense pile is left medium to high. Unfortunately, the wool used in these rugs is sometimes taken from skins rather than shorn from live animals. This yields a very poor quality yarn that doesn't react well with certain dyestuffs. Handling the pile will give you a good clue as to what kind of yarn has been used in a particular rug—poor quality wool will feel lifeless.

The standard sizes for Meshed rugs are 12 by 9 and 14 by 10 feet, although some square rugs are also available. They're in the medium price range among Iranian rugs.

The finest rugs from the Meshed area are known as Isfahans. However, these pieces bear no resemblance to the rugs that are actually made in the city of Isfahan—there are great differences not only in the colors, but also in the quality of the weaving and in the material used. Khorasan is another name you might run across when you're looking at rugs from this area—Meshed is the capital of the province of Khorasan, and in the past its rugs were often called by that name. SEE *Mud.*

Meshkin (Mishkin, Meshgin)   These double-wefted rugs from the Herez district of Iran are modern adaptations of older Caucasian-style rugs. In the typical Meshkin, three octagonal medallions are worked in Turkish knots on a semi-open, geometrically patterned field (PLATE xxx). However, unlike the Caucasian models, the Meshkin is woven on cotton warps and in earth tones rather than reds.

Meshkins are some of the least expensive Iranian rugs, but fewer and fewer are now being exported. Meshkins are made in a full range of sizes, from mats to room-sized carpets, as well as in very narrow runners. However, they're not recommended for high-traffic areas; it's particularly important not to use the narrow runners on flights of stairs. SEE *Ardebil.*

Copies of Meshkin rugs are made in India. Ironically, some of these are more costly than the originals.

Milâs (Melâs)   Small rugs, up to 8 by 5 feet, are still woven in traditional designs in this part of western Turkey. Milâs prayer rugs often have a distinctive greenish-yellow color and an abstract, somewhat naively rendered geometric pattern (PLATE XL). Earth tones—particularly shades of brown, gray, and yellow—are also used.

Milâs rugs are of fair to medium quality (they usually have about 80 or 90 knots per square inch) and are lower in price than most other Turkish rugs. Many of the rugs from this area are made in the seccade size (approximately 6½ by 3¾ feet), although some are available in sizes up to 10 by 8 feet.

Milâs designs are now copied in Romania.

Mud (Moud) These rugs, produced in the province of Khorasan in northeastern Iran, are finely woven, with a short pile. Their design generally consists of an intricate version of the Herati pattern on a white or a blue field, with or without central medallions (PLATE XV).

Rugs from Mud have cotton warps and double wefts. They come in sizes that range from 5 by 3½ to 18 by 12 feet, and they're usually fairly expensive. In fact, the name Mud is sometimes used to describe the best-quality rugs of the whole Khorasan district. SEE *Meshed.*

Nain Although this Iranian weaving center has only been active for the past fifty years, it produces very finely woven rugs. Most Nains have over 400 knots per square inch—and the best ones can have over 600 knots per square inch. Nain weavers use a number of patterns, although the Shah Abbas is the most common. Occasionally Nain designs will also contain flower buds and animals. All these patterns are worked in soft colors on very fine cotton warps, with silk outlining (PLATE II).

Nains are usually made in one standard size, 5¼ by 3½ feet, but they can also occasionally be found in smaller sizes or in full-room sizes. Obviously, one of the most important things to consider when you're looking at these rugs is the knot count. In addition, although Nains are usually "square," it's a good idea to check the shape of the rug for any irregularities by carefully folding it in half and comparing the dimensions. SEE *Isfahan, Kashan, Qum.*

Peking These classic carpets were once made only in the area near the Chinese capital. Although rugs are still woven in Peking, the name is now used for all rugs that have been made in the traditional design, regardless of which Chinese weaving center they actually come from.

The Peking pattern usually consists of a single round medallion, or several medallions, arranged symetrically on an open field, although other basic design elements can also be used (PLATES XLIII, XLIV, XLVII, XLVIII). Traditionally, Peking rugs were woven in a limited number of colors, including classic blue shades that are usually associated with Chinese weaving and ceramics. Today, however, they're woven in a wide variety of colors. In addition, all Peking rugs are embossed to add depth to the design.

Peking rugs come in a broad range of qualities, including some that have been handtufted rather than handwoven. They're available in standard American sizes, from 5 by 3 to 18 by 12 feet. These rugs provide good value, although they're not necessarily good investments.

Because their designs are relatively simple, Peking copies form the basis of the Indian weaving industry, just as Bokhara patterns are the staples of Pakistani weavers. Copies of Chinese designs are particularly common among lower quality Indian rugs. Peking patterns are also woven in Taiwan (PLATE XLVI).

Qashqa'i (Kashkai, Gashgai) The Qashqa'i are a tribe of south Persian nomads who trade their finely woven, geometrically patterned rugs in the city of Shiraz. Today the name has come to be used for the best quality rugs from the whole Shiraz area. Qashqa'is are brightly colored in reddish browns and blues. The typical design usually has a diamond-shaped center and a richly detailed background filled with small geometric figures or stylized flowers. The prayer rug is also very popular among Qashqa'i weavers.

Qashqa'i rugs generally have wool warps. They can be easily identified by their red wool wefts and by a selvedge that wraps the sides of the rug with two or more colors of yarn. These rugs can be very finely woven and when their pile is clipped short the finished rug will be rather stiff. Qashqa'is are made only in smaller sizes, up to 8 by 5 feet. They're among the most expensive rugs from the Shiraz area and their prices can sometimes even rival those of the more formal city rugs. SEE *Shiraz, Yalameh.*

Qashqa'i designs are now reproduced by Indian weavers. These rugs will probably be copied more and more often in the future by both Indian and Pakistani weavers.

Qum (Quom, Kum) Rugmaking was only established in the ancient holy city of Iran during the last half century. Since the area has no deeply rooted weaving tradition, its designs are borrowed from those of Kashan, Tabriz, Isfahan, and other older weaving centers; some of these adaptations are combinations of elements from various patterns, and so they might be said to be original (PLATE XIII). The Shah Abbas pattern, with or without a central medallion, is popular among the weavers in Qum, as is an all-over pattern of repeating botehs, a garden design, and pattern called Zel-i-Sultan that looks like a small bouquet or a turban on a head. However, since so many designs are used in the area, color and weaving technique are really the only constants.

Carpets from Qum are woven using a technique very similar to that used in Kashan, and the wool is usually of good quality. Shades of red and blue are the most common field colors, and a good deal of white is used in the designs. The weaving is done on cotton warps, and the finished pieces range in size from 7 by 4 to 14 by 10 feet.

Qum is also famous for its silk pile rugs. These may have warps or wefts (or both) in silk; obviously, a rug that's all silk will be much more expensive. Silk pieces come in sizes from 2½ by 1½ feet to 8 by 5 feet, with 5¼ by 3½ feet the most common. These rugs are produced in traditional designs and in interesting hunting patterns that are quite suitable for hanging. Naturally, the knot count is critical in assessing silk rugs because it can vary a great deal, even among finely woven pieces. One of these rugs might seem very handsome when you look at it by itself—but it might be less impressive next to another fine silk carpet.

Both wool and silk rugs from Qum are expensive, but the silk pieces are at the top of the price scale. As you would expect, the silk rugs are also the most suitable for investors. SEE *Nain, Isfahan, Kashan.*

Despite the fact that rugs from Qum can't really be called original designs, there are still Pakistani and Indian versions of them on the market (PLATE xxv). When you're looking at these copies, it's wise to compare samples from each country against the Iranian original.

Sarouk (Saruk) The Sarouk is the best quality rug from the Arak weaving district of central Iran, an area that was once called Sultanabad. For over half a century, Sarouks have been woven in a distinctive design that consists of brightly colored detached floral sprays, with or without a medallion, placed throughout a red or blue field and surrounded by a simple main border in a contrasting color (PLATE xxiii). One variant of the standard Sarouk design is the small repeated boteh pattern called the Seraband, or Mir (PLATE xxiv). In addition, Sarouks are also occasionally woven in patterns that resemble the open field Kerman, and Sarouks destined for the European market are worked in a classic intertwining medallion design (PLATE iv). These are sometimes called Jozan Sarouks because of their resemblance to the rugs produced in the nearby town of Jozan.

Sarouks are woven on cotton warps, and sometimes you'll be able to identify them by their distinctive blue wefts. The knotting can be very fine, and the wool is of excellent quality, so the finished carpet is quite hard-wearing. The pile, which was once clipped quite close, is now left somewhat longer in deference to the tastes of the American market.

At one time, many Sarouk rugs were painted with dye after the rugs had arrived in the U.S. This process was intended to intensify certain colors, which wouldn't be produced in deep enough shades in the original pile yarns. Today, with the use of modern chrome dyes, it's no longer necessary to paint the fields of Sarouks, and the practice has died out.

Sarouks are available in many sizes, from mats to large room-sized pieces. Sarouks are expensive, but their resale value is very steady. However, when you're considering these rugs, it's important to make a careful comparison of the knot counts because some lesser quality Mahal rugs have been represented as Sarouks. SEE *Arak, Seraband, Jozan, Melayer.*

Indian rugs that bear a strong resemblance to Sarouks are now available on the international market. So are Pakistani Sarouks in a variety of field colors and a good range of sizes, including runners.

Senneh (Sehna, Senna, Sinneh)   This town in the Iranian province of Kurdistan has the same name that's given to the Persian knotting technique—although the weavers in Senneh rarely use the Senneh knot. Their rugs are finely woven on cotton foundations with a distinctive single weft and a short pile, which make for a comparatively lightweight pile rug. Senneh is also known for its flat-woven kilim rugs.

The most commonly used design element in Senneh rugs is the Herati, which is often incorporated into larger patterns formed by variously colored concentric, diamond-shaped medallions. Other common designs include a repeating pattern of small botehs or small stylized flowers. All these patterns are surrounded by a typical Persian border composed of a main stripe with two guard stripes. Blue and white are the primary background colors, and red is used for accents.

These very durable rugs are among the more expensive carpets made in Iran. Unfortunately, current production is limited to a few throw-rug sizes and even fewer room sizes. SEE *Mud.*

Senneh rugs have proven somewhat difficult to copy. Their finely drawn designs don't lend themselves to the Indian weaving technique, which, as a rule, contains fewer knots per square inch.

Serab (Sarab, Sarap)   This village in the Herez district of Iran produces rugs in shades of rust, camel, dark blue, green, and ivory woven on cotton foundations. There is generally very little variation in color from one rug to another, and the quality of the weaving is also quite uniform.

The typical Serab design is a pattern of repeated hexagonal or

171

diamond-shaped medallions, often connected so that they seem set along a pole (PLATE XXXVI). The standard width of a Serab rug is around 3½ feet, and the length ranges from 6 to 12 feet. These carpets are both durable and moderately priced. SEE *Herez, Karaje.*

Seraband (Saraband, Serrebend)   The few rugs that are now woven in this part of Iran's Arak district continue to feature the age-old design of rows of botehs arranged on a deep red or blue (and sometimes ivory, gold, or green) field, surrounded by borders worked in white and decorated with angular vines and stylized flowers. The prefix "Mir" is often used to describe this classic "paisley" design, in which the stem of the boteh faces in a different direction from row to row. This kind of alternation is found in very few other districts, although it's used in rugs from nearby Sarouk and in runners from the Hamadan area.

Seraband rugs are usually of medium quality or better, but they're only available in a limited range of small sizes. They're among the moderately priced Iranian rugs. SEE *Sarouk, Hamadan.*

The classic Seraband pattern appears in many rugs from India, and is particularly common in runners, a size to which it adapts well. It's also widely copied in machinemade rugs.

Shiraz   The capital of Fars province in southern Iran serves as a collection point for the rugs made by nomadic tribes in this area. Rugs are also produced by villagers in the region, as well as in rug factories. In the city of Shiraz itself there are a number of weaving schools.

The brightly colored, geometrically designed Shiraz rugs are made on woolen foundations and are usually single wefted, often with a distinctive dark fringe (PLATE XVII). The Shiraz district also produces more flat-woven rugs than any other part of Iran; these kilims are worked in the standard Shiraz designs that feature a column of large medallions (PLATE XXXI).

Shiraz rugs are worked in a medium pile height, usually in small sizes, although larger pieces do appear now and then. The quality of these rugs can vary from coarse to medium, and some are quite loosely knotted. You'll notice that the patterns become more obscure in the more coarsely woven pieces. Shiraz rugs tend to be reasonably priced, although those that are more finely woven will naturally cost more. SEE *Qashqa'i, Yalameh, Afshar.*

Indian weavers are now reproducing a number of Shiraz designs, and the odds are that they'll be copying even more of them in the future.

Shirvan   This type of rug was once made only in the southeastern Caucasus, but today Shirvans are produced in state factories throughout the Transcaucasian Soviet Republics. These rugs come in a wide range of colors, with blue and red used for the backgrounds. They're also available in a wide range of geometric designs. The most common incorporates either a neat, tight, repeating pattern or one or more medallions in the shape of a flattened star. Other common designs feature stylized ram's horns and birds. Prayer rug patterns are also quite popular.

Shirvans are fairly finely woven, on cotton foundations, rather than on the wool foundations that were used in the past. Because of the tariffs imposed on Russian imports, these rugs command very high prices, but since they're only available in small sizes, they don't tend to be prohibitively expensive.

Shirvan designs are widely copied in India and Pakistan, often in finer weaves than the originals. In many cases, the colors have also been modified (PLATES LII, LIII).

Tabriz   These popular carpets from the extreme northwest of Iran, near the Turkish border, can be recognized by their Turkish knotting, which is worked with a hook on fully stacked warps. Another distinctive feature is the modern colors in which they're made—burnt orange, persimmon, light blue, and green, to mention only a few. This color palette is fairly standard, and it's interesting to note that—at least as far as rugs destined for America are concerned—it doesn't usually include any deep reds.

Rugs from Tabriz are made in various patterns, including garden designs and all-over hunting, or animal, designs. These may incorporate a medallion, with or without an open field (PLATE I).

173

The Shah Abbas pattern is also commonly used.

Tabriz rugs are made on cotton foundations in a range of qualities, from fairly coarse to extremely fine. In average-quality rugs, heavy wefting is used to provide body and durability. The pile height of the finer rugs is lower than the pile in other qualities.

Tabriz rugs are available in as great a range of sizes as it's possible to find in Iran. However, since they have a tendency to be a bit crooked, it's wise to check the straightness of the edges of any rugs you're considering and see how even they are in dimension from edge to edge along the length and the width.

Because of its popularity, the Tabriz carpet is now being reproduced in India in a full range of American sizes. Indo-Tabriz rugs can be either exact copies or adaptations of the original designs (PLATE XII). Balkan weavers, particularly those in Romania and Yugoslavia, are also copying Tabriz patterns.

Tekke   The Tekke were a nomadic Turkoman tribe whose rugs were collected at Bokhara in Central Asia. Today, Tekke Bokharas are made in state-run factories throughout the Soviet Republic of Turkmenistan. Like other Bokhara rugs, Tekke pieces are worked in the classic design of rows and columns of guls on a rich red or burgundy field; however, the gul itself is different from that used in the rugs of other Turkoman tribes. In addition, Tekke rugs also feature a distinctive windowpane design in which the guls are connected to each other by very thin lines.

Tekke Bokharas are finely woven on wool warps in sizes up to 9 by 6. These rugs are beautifully made and are of the very best quality—and so they're also very expensive. SEE *Bokhara.*

Tekke Bokharas are produced in Iran by weavers who have migrated across the Russian border. The Tekke pattern is also incorporated into much of the weaving from India and Pakistan, but in most cases it's radically modified and combined with other Turkoman design elements.

Veramin   Weavers in this village in north-central Iran usually work their rugs in the Minahani pattern. Other common designs are a repeating vase and a pattern that features plant and animal figures. All these designs are set against a dark blue background.

Veramins are made on cotton foundations, and the weaving is generally very good. These fine quality rugs are available in sizes up to 10 by 7 feet. They're quite expensive, but they're also very good investments.

Veramin designs are now copied in India.

Yaçibedir (Yağci-bedir)   These Turkish village rugs are woven on woolen foundations, usually with a dark blue ground and deep red top colors (PLATE XXXVIII). The standard design features an elongated hexagonal medallion with stepped spandrels at either end of the field. The field itself is usually filled with stars or large stylized birds.

Yaçibedir rugs are worked with a relatively short pile, mostly in the seccade (6½ by 3¾ feet) or the ceyrek (4½ by 2¾ feet) size. Narrow runners are also quite common. All these carpets are moderately priced.

Yalameh   These geometrically designed rugs are made by nomadic weavers in the Fars province of southern Iran. Yalamehs are woven with good quality wool in a medium pile height on woolen warps in dark but bright colors, usually with white accents. A diamond medallion pattern is often used, with the individual medallions connected so that they seem set along a pole (PLATE XVI). Other common styles include a garden pattern and several all-over repeated designs. All these patterns feature a well-covered field, with spandrels in contrasting colors at each end.

The most common sizes for Yalamehs are 3 by 2 foot mats and 5 by 3 foot throw rugs. Larger sizes are available, but not in any significant quantity. The repeating medallion pattern is particularly suited to medium-sized runners. Yalamehs are among the moderately priced Iranian rugs. SEE *Shiraz, Qashqa'i.*

A few Indian rugs are now woven in the Yalameh style.

Yezd   Weavers in this town to the northwest of Kerman in Iran produce short-pile copies of Kashan designs. These are made with cream backgrounds, and they have fewer knots than the Kashan originals. In the past, Yezd weavers preferred to copy Kerman patterns, and some of these are also still made. They have the medium to high pile you'll find in Kermans, but only two wefts instead of the three used in the originals.

Yezds are somewhat less expensive than the Kashan rugs on which they're modeled, not only because the weaving isn't as fine but also because lesser quality wool, which tends to be somewhat pulpy, is used for the pile. Yezds are generally available in large sizes. SEE *Kashan, Kerman.*

Yomut (Yamout)   The Yomut were a nomadic Turkoman tribe whose rugs were collected at Bokhara, in central Asia. Today, Yomut rugs are made in state-run factories throughout the Soviet Republic of Turkmenistan. Like other Bokharas, Yomuts are woven on wool warps in the familiar pattern of rows and columns of guls. However, Yomut Bokharas are distinctive not only because of their own variation of the gul design, but also because the red Yomut background colors have a brown or purple cast.

Yomuts are woven in small to medium room sizes. The pile height is kept low, and the finished rugs are quite supple. Like other Russian rugs, Yomuts tend to be rather expensive. SEE *Bokhara.*

Yomut designs are copied in India and Pakistan, but with a higher pile. Because these copies are made on cotton warps, they're often more finely woven than the originals.

LESS COMMON RUG TYPES

Although the directory in this chapter includes all the major rug types that are available in the United States, there are, of course, many others that you may hear of, see, or even own. These rugs can come from any one of hundreds of villages that produce only a limited number of rugs, or they may be slightly older rugs from once popular weaving centers whose rug industry has declined or disappeared. They may even be rugs that have been labeled with an old, but inaccurate name, one that has persisted simply because of its frequent use.

A Directory of Major Rug Types

The rugs listed below have been divided into very general groups and provided with a reference to a rug type in the directory or a term in the glossary that will help you get a general idea of how to identify them. If you can't find a name on this list and you know that the rug in question isn't a new one, you can consult the bibliography for other books that will give you information on how to proceed. If, on the other hand, you know that you're looking at a new rug and you can't find the name in the directory, the glossary, or this supplemental list, then it may very well be a private label, probably from India or Pakistan. If so, it's up to you to ask questions about it!

Rug Type	Identification Reference
IRAN	
Bakshaish	HEREZ
Bibibaff	BAKHTIARI
Birjand	MUD
Feraghan	ARAK
Gorevan	HEREZ
Kermanshah	KERMAN
Khamseh	SHIRAZ
Khorasan	MESHED
Lilihan	SAROUK
Luristan	SHIRAZ
Mosul	HAMADAN
Mushkabad	MAHAL
Ravar (Lavar)	KERMAN
Saveh	QUM

Rug Type	Identification Reference
IRAN *(cont'd)*	
Semnan	MESHED
Serapi	HEREZ
Sultanabad	ARAK
Tafresh	HAMADAN
Teheran	VERAMIN, ISFAHAN
Viss	ARDEBIL
Zenjan	HAMADAN
TURKEY	
Akhisar	YAÇIBEDIR
Bergama	YAÇIBEDIR
Canakkale	DOSEMEALTI
Kirshehir	KONIA
Kumpaki	HEREKE
Mudjur	KEYSERI
Oushak	GHIORDES
Panderma	GHIORDES
Sivas	TABRIZ, KEYSERI
AFGHANISTAN	
Mauri	AFGHAN

A Directory of Major Rug Types

Rug Type	Identification Reference
CAUCASUS	
Chi Chi	SHIRVAN
Daghestan	SHIRVAN
Derbent	KAZAK
Gendje	SHIRVAN
Kabistan	SHIRVAN
Karabagh	KAZAK
Kuba	SHIRVAN
TURKESTAN	
Khiva	AFGHAN
Pende	BOKHARA
Salor	BOKHARA

CHAPTER IX

CARING FOR
YOUR ORIENTAL RUG

ORIENTAL RUGS CAN BE QUITE STURDY, AND THEY can keep their beauty for a very long time— but only if you treat them with the respect they deserve. You should give your Oriental rug as much care as you'd give any other valuable object you might own. The notion that a lot of wear is good for a rug is a dangerously simple way of looking at things, and it ignores the fact that any rug, old or new, must be properly maintained. Don't forget that the reputation Orientals have for being hard-wearing and long-lasting was built up in an era when the style of living was very different than it is today.

In the past, Oriental rugs were usually owned by people who could afford larger homes and had comparatively smaller families and more domestic help. Their rugs got less use and were well cared for, so well that they were often given a vacation in the summer—cold storage. Nowadays, Orientals are owned by families who give them more use, not just in the winter but year-round. Their rugs are subjected to the rigors of air conditioning and central heating, worked over by humidifiers and dehumidifiers, and exposed to the effects of new chemicals and foreign substances—

all in addition to the general wear-and-tear of modern family life.

It should be obvious, then, that Oriental rugs aren't indestructible. In fact, the task of preventive maintenance begins almost as soon as you buy your rug. But this doesn't mean that caring for an Oriental rug has to be a burden. You'll be pleasantly surprised to find that the wool that makes up the pile of your rug is more resistant to soils than any synthetic fiber. So if you take the right precautions and exercise a bit of common sense—and if you followed the guidelines in this book when you bought your rug—you won't have to consider major maintenance costs and repairs for many years. Right now, your concerns will be selecting the right pads for your rug, cleaning it when it gets soiled, and keeping an eye on the general use it's getting.

PADS

Unfortunately, many people overlook the importance of selecting the right pads, or cushions, when they're buying a rug. This is a mistake because pads have a specific job to do, and you shouldn't underestimate their importance. Even if pads are "thrown in" with the sale, make sure that they're the right ones for the rug and how it will be used. The wrong pad, even if it's free, is no bargain.

The basic function of padding is to protect the rug from the pressure that's applied to it. This is why it's important to have the right kind of padding. If the padding is too soft, the foundation of the rug will stretch when you walk on it or set furniture on it, and the rug will wear faster. A pad also serves to muffle noise, it helps to keep the rug from moving, and it elevates the rug to make the pile surface look deeper. Finally, using the proper pad will provide an air space between the carpet and the floor, and that will make vacuuming the rug much easier and more effective.

A dealer who has a completely stocked showroom will be able to show you several different types of pads. One that's generally recommended is made of a combination of animal hair and jute. This weighs from 40 to 56 ounces a square yard and has a thin rubber coating on both sides.

Another good type is solid sponge rubber. This is probably the best all-around padding you can buy, especially if there's anyone at home who might be allergic to the hair and jute mats. Sponge rubber mats are usually a quarter of an inch thick, but they also come in a thinner gauge that's used under scatter rugs to keep them in place—a safety precaution that shouldn't be taken lightly.

If you're going to buy a sponge-rubber pad, be sure that it actually *is* sponge rubber. Remember, sponge rubber isn't the same as ripple rubber, the kind of padding that's used under wall-to-wall carpeting. Also steer clear of pads made of foam rubber or synthetic materials. They tend to compress almost completely, so they don't give your rugs very much protection.

CLEANING

Dirt has been defined as matter out of place. Sand, lovely on a beach, is destructive when it's imbedded into the fibers of a rug. Oil and grease are effective lubricants for machinery, but when they're spilled or tracked on rugs they attract other soils. Gritty dirt may work its way down into the pile of a rug and cut into the fibers; grease will eventually penetrate and saturate the pile material. These kinds of soils aren't always apparent at first, but if you wait until they become visible, it may be too late to prevent permanent damage. That's why you should stick to a weekly vacuuming routine, whether or not your rug looks "dirty." And every few years your efforts should be backed up by a professional shampooing. It may seem obvious, but it's worth saying—a clean rug looks better and lasts longer.

When you vacuum your rug, do it *slowly*. If you can, try to use a beater-bar type of machine. This gently reproduces the action of an old-fashioned carpet beater, loosening the soils that have become imbedded in the rug and drawing them out. However, if you have a very thin or fragile carpet, it may not be able to stand up to the action of the beater bars, and in this case you'll have to use another kind of vacuum cleaner. Whatever method you choose for your weekly cleaning, it's also a good idea to keep a carpet sweeper on hand for any daily attention that might be necessary.

You may not want to do this every week, but you'll find that the most effective way to clean your carpet is to slowly vacuum it from the *back* with a beater-bar machine. You'll be astounded at the amount of grit that will fall out. This method of cleaning also draws out very short, light-absorbing bits of yarn that can otherwise dull the luster of the carpet. When you've completely vacuumed the back of the rug, a quick cleaning of the face will bring about a dramatic change in the appearance of the rug.

Shampooing a rug is also important, not only because it will thoroughly remove any dirt or soils that your vacuuming may have missed, but also because it will put moisture back into the carpet. This may sound odd at first; after all, too much moisture can make your rug mildewed and cause permanent damage. On the other hand, it's also true that the low humidity in many of today's houses can make rugs brittle and dry—and this can cause just as much damage.

If you want to shampoo the rug yourself, you'll find a number of synthetic detergents on the market that will do the job. When you're using them, the trick is not to saturate the rug and not to allow the foundation to become wet. When this happens, you may have difficulty getting the rug thoroughly dry, and if it stays damp for too long, the fibers may become mildewed, dry rot may attack the foundation, and the colors might bleed. This is why it's usually a better idea to have the shampooing done professionally. After all, a professional cleaner has the facilities to clean each rug according to its particular needs, and he'll also be able to dry the rugs quickly and safely.

You should choose a professional cleaner just as carefully as you would a dealer. As a matter of fact, many dealers also provide a cleaning service, and this kind of set-up is likely to be your best choice, particularly if the same dealer sold you your rug. After all, it's in the dealer's interest for you to continue to be happy with your rug, so he'll give you the best possible service.

Be wary of "freelance" rug-cleaning operations that aren't affiliated with a dealership. Many of these companies specialize in cleaning wall-to-wall carpets, and they may not always be familiar with Orientals. The bargain-priced cleaning they give your rug may not be such a bargain when you consider the possible damage that could result. Remember that an effective professional cleaning can't be done in your home—the rug must be taken to an establishment that has all the equipment needed to give it a thorough washing and drying.

Of course, in between professional cleanings, you'll have to deal with stains and spills yourself. When accidents happen, try to remedy the situation as soon as possible. If there's a spill, immediately absorb as much of the liquid as you can by blotting it with a paper towel or a soft cloth. Don't rub or brush at it. This could only spread the damage and disturb and distort the pile.

Don't immediately attack stains with water. Especially in the case of an oil-based stain, you're always safer with a "dry" (petroleum-based) cleaning solvent. This kind of solvent evaporates, so even if it doesn't work, you won't have caused any further damage. Some stains may also respond to a neutral detergent, the kind you'd use to wash delicate clothing. But be careful when you use them! Always pretest a detergent on an inconspicuous part of the rug, and remember not to get the rug too wet. If the rug does become damp, you'll have to make sure that it's thoroughly and quickly dried. Try using a hand-held hair dryer on the wet patch or cover the area with towels and weight them down so they'll soak up all the extra moisture. Another trick to try, if the weather cooperates, is to dry the rug in bright, hot sunlight.

Above all, if you have any doubts about how to handle a spill, be sure to consult a professional rug cleaner. Remember that the haphazard attempts you might make to remove a spot could create a permanent stain or destroy the pile of the rug.

MAINTENANCE

One general preventive measure you can take to even the wear on your carpet is to reverse its direction every now and then. Giving the rug a 180-degree turn will cut down the use of any given area up to fifty percent. In other words, it can double the life of the rug. You might also consider changing the placement of your furniture from time to time. After all, if the furniture arrangement stays the same, so will the areas where traffic flows—and these areas will naturally suffer more damage.

Another way to reduce the wear on your rug is to store it during the summer. But don't get carried away with this! Remember, you're supposed to be enjoying your rug. You certainly can't get much satisfaction from something that's rolled up and stored away for most of the year! However, if you do have to store your rug for an extended period of time, make sure that it's cleaned first. And if you're storing the rug at home be sure to treat it with a moth repellent. Then roll the rug against the direction of the lay of the nap so that it forms a tight cylinder. Most rugs have supple foundations, so you may be able to make a more compact bundle by folding your rug in half, or even folding it lengthwise, before you roll it. Once it's rolled up, be sure that the place you've chosen to store it is completely dry.

Whether your rug is in use or in storage, you should be on the alert for moths and carpet beetles. These insects can devour the wool pile of a carpet with such relish that I sometimes wonder if they aren't old rug dealers reincarnated. A thorough professional cleaning is the best way to prevent moth damage because the washing removes the larvae and the hot drying destroys the eggs. Insecticides and mothproofers are also efficient (any petroleum distillate will kill moths and their larvae), but it's more effective to use them after the rug has had a thorough cleaning.

Another problem that's becoming more and more common is dry rot. This is caused by mildew, a fungus that thrives on the cotton in the foundation of most rugs. More often than not, an indoor plant is the "root" of this unfortunate situation. Unless there's some air circulation between the plant container and the floor covering, condensation will form, and the dampness soon leads to dry rot. It can be very costly to repair this kind of damage, and in many cases it simply isn't worthwhile, even if the mildew has only spread over a small area.

REPAIR

One of the best ways to protect your rug is to give it a careful inspection every now and then. The fringes and selvedges are usually the weakest parts of the rug, so they're often the first to show signs of wear. When you see even the slightest evidence of this, you should consult a company that's qualified to repair the rug. Otherwise, the body of the carpet may also become damaged.

When you're inspecting your rug, you may also notice an occasional white knot or thread on the face. This isn't a serious situation. It's quite normal for many tied ends in the rug's foundation to be buried in the pile during the weaving process instead of protruding on the back of the carpet. In time, as the pile becomes compressed from use, some of these knots may show. When this happens, they can be clipped down, but only by someone who knows what he's doing. In many cases, it's easier to simply touch them up with a dye that matches the color of the surrounding knots. Again, this should only be done by a professional.

Another sign you may notice when you're inspecting your rug is a curled edge or a wrinkle. In some weaving centers the width of a rug is temporarily reinforced by attaching a beam to the side as the rug is woven. When this technique isn't used, the edges of the rug may be pulled in. This problem, which often isn't apparent until the rug is removed from the loom, can sometimes be corrected by stretching or blocking, and in more serious cases, the selvedges may be sewn out invisibly so that the rug can lie flat. Unfortunately, these corrective measures may have to be renewed over the years. It's important not to allow curled edges and wrinkles to go untended. If you do, they'll cause premature and unnecessary wear on the part that's uneven, and this area may eventually tear.

The correction of all these problems—and any others that might arise—should be entrusted to a reputable company that's qualified to repair Oriental rugs. You'll find that a rug dealer who offers cleaning services will often have the facilities to repair rugs as well. This kind of establishment would be the best to start with when you're looking for someone to work on your rug.

If you aren't familiar with the people who'll be doing the repairs, visit the workroom and watch them in action. Ask to see some completed jobs, and ask questions about how they would repair your rug. Insist that any repairs be done in the same technique that was used when the rug was originally made, if this is at all possible.

Above all, don't allow repairs to be carried out by machine. The only time this might be acceptable is when an artificial fringe must be sewn on—and even then it's often preferable to fray out or overcast worn ends instead. All too often, the ends and sides of rugs are literally chopped off before ready-made fringes are sewn on. This type of repair may produce a temporary improvement in looks, but it also permanently decreases the value of the rug.

Of course, it's wise to do some comparison shopping before you choose someone to repair your rug, but remember that you're inquiring about a very specialized service. The cost shouldn't be the only factor to consider when you make your decision. A competent job of repairing and restoring, although expensive, will pay for itself in the years to come. On the other hand, a poor repair job will cost you immediately—either in further repairs or in permanent damage to the rug.

CHAPTER X

RESALE, TRADE, & INVESTMENT

THE MOST IMPORTANT REASON FOR BUYING A RUG is to use it and thoroughly enjoy it. But, beyond that, it seems unrealistic to ignore the fact that Oriental rugs are also bought as investments, as hedges against inflation. And even though this may not have been uppermost in your mind when you bought your rug, it makes sense to give it some thought. After all, someday you might want to sell your rug or trade it in.

The values of Oriental rugs can change dramatically, and your rug's current market value may be quite different from the price you first paid for it. Of course, you can find out how much your rug is worth by doing some research on your own, but the easiest (and most reliable) way is to have it appraised by a professional. Be sure to choose your appraiser with as much caution as you chose your dealer; he should be an expert in the field. Be especially wary of general fine arts appraisers—all too often they won't have enough familiarity with Oriental rugs to give you a reliable estimate.

Once you have gotten an appraisal, make sure you have a written record of it, along with a photograph of the rug, just as you would for any other valuables you own. Keep these, along with a copy of the record-keeping form in the Appendix, in a secure place outside your home, preferably in a safe deposit box. That way, if your rug should ever be stolen or damaged, your insurance claim will be far more easily settled.

And while you're getting yourself so well organized, why not make sure that your insurance is actually protecting your rug. In many cases, a basic homeowner's policy simply doesn't offer enough coverage. However, for a small additional charge you can itemize an Oriental rug on a so-called fine arts floater. In addition to providing all the coverage you need, this will also eliminate the necessity of estimating an appraisal if your rug should happen to be damaged or stolen.

RESALE AND TRADE

Remember that when you're selling and trading your own rugs, the appraisal value should only be used as a point of reference. It's wise to keep in mind the fact that you're offering a much more limited selection in terms of size, color, and design than any commercial rug dealer. It's unreasonable for you to expect a retail price for your rug—after all, there was a difference between the price the dealer originally paid for your rug and the price at which it was sold to you. It may also be unreasonable, since you aren't in the business, for you to expect to get a wholesale price. However, if you're armed with a realistic appraisal of your rug's current value, you can ask for a significant percentage of that value.

In addition, remember that when you're dealing with new Oriental rugs, it takes a number of years for inflation to catch up, for the resale price of the rug to match or top the original sale price. In the meantime, you've been enjoying your rug—but you've also been using it. Obviously, it won't be new when it's resold, so it may not be worth as much as a new rug from the same source. What you should hope for is that between the time you bought the rug and the time you sell it, the rug will have acquired a special appeal or become scarce, thus increasing in value.

You can expect to get more out of your rug if it's traded than if it's sold. Dealers tend to be more generous in a trade; they can afford to give away a little more of their profit. It's something like trading in your old car when you buy a new one—and the same kind of comparative shopping applies.

Go to a dealer and find out how much a rug will cost with a trade and without, and then look around a bit. Remember that rugs can have different values in different circumstances. For any number of reasons, one dealer may want your rug more than another dealer does. Some dealers have a reputation for selling used rugs. Their stock turns over quickly, and they may need your rug to fill in the gaps. This type of dealer is probably also more knowledgeable when it comes to determining the current value of used rugs. Often, dealers who concentrate on selling new rugs simply aren't in touch with the market in old or used ones.

One final word of caution: when you settle on a dealer and trade in your rug, it's crucial that you like the new rug you're trading for, that you're not just accepting the "best" deal for your old rug. You must be happy with your new selection too—or else you may find yourself looking for another trade much sooner than you expected.

INVESTMENT

We're all painfully aware of the rising rate of inflation and the fact that dollars simply don't buy as much today as they did yesterday. For these reasons, rugs that have a resale value are considered a viable hedge against inflation, an "investment." At the same time, it's also true that the value of used merchandise depends on how much merchandise was originally produced, any special qualities it might have, how well it was cared for, how well it was made, how long ago it was made, and—most important—how much of a demand there is for it.

Most investment in Orientals involves antique and semi-antique rugs, not only because the supplies are limited but also because the resale value of good pieces has been established through years of selling and trading. Older Iranian rugs are particularly sought after as investments, and so are old rugs from the Caucasus and Turkestan (now both part of the Soviet Union) and old Turkish village rugs.

The market value of older Orientals is determined by a number of factors, but if I had to give just one specific reason why some older rugs are so much more valuable it would have to be their color. Newer rugs can be just as finely woven as antique and semi-antique rugs, but their colors are never quite the same as the appealing shades produced over the years by the mellowing of the dyes in older rugs. However, this difference isn't as simple as it might seem; appraising the value of an older rug requires much more than an eye for color. Many old rugs, mellow as they may be, are worn or damaged, and aren't particularly valuable.

Since good-quality older rugs are becoming quite scarce, more and more buyers are becoming interested in investing in new Orientals, and it seems certain that the investment opportunities in new rugs can only increase in the years to come. However, if you're buying a new rug with this in mind it's absolutely essential to make a careful selection. Buying new rugs for investment can be a risky proposition, for a number of reasons.

When we talk about "investing" in new Oriental rugs it's important to remember that we're referring to supply and demand. Basically, we're concerned about someone's opinion, about what the market will demand and value in the years to come. Demand—subject as it is to changes in taste, to shifting preferences in color and design—is hard to project. For example, kilims, which were quite reasonably priced just a few years ago when their reputation among collectors was minimal, have become much more valuable as their popularity has increased.

Another important aspect of demand is its international scope. The United States was once the chief importer of Oriental rugs, but when the use of wall-to-wall carpeting became popular here, Europe and the Middle East maintained their interest in Orientals and moved into a dominant position in the market. Today, their greater purchasing power has only strengthened that position. These days, Americans must compete with buyers from rich foreign countries all over the world. For example, West Germans buy many more Orientals than Americans do, and investors from the oil-producing countries are also an important force in the market. The situation is further complicated by the fact that the supply of rugs from certain countries—notably Iran and Russia—is steadily declining.

When you're considering the investment value of a new Oriental rug, there are certain basic factors to keep in mind. Obviously, if a certain type of rug is only made in small quantities, then that type will be harder to find—and there's a better chance that the rugs will hold their value in the future. However, these rugs should also be of good quality and in styles and colors that have an appeal in the marketplace. In general, if you're concerned about investment, it's wise to keep your choice of a rug somewhat traditional in terms of color and style; the classics offer a bit more protection against changes in taste because they never seem to go out of style. In addition, if you're buying primarily for investment purposes, you should get the very best quality rug you can afford.

Finally, you should consider the reputations of the various rug-producing countries. Obviously, no one can predict with certainty, but it's fairly safe to assume, based on history and experience, that the better products of Iran will appreciate at a higher rate than rugs from other weaving centers. To put it quite simply, there's a mystique about Iranian rugs, and even relatively poorly made, used rugs from that country command a fair resale price. Although the status and quality of Iranian rugs have a good deal to do with this, it's difficult to pin down all the factors involved—and it's possible that the situation will change, particularly since the quality of some Iranian rugs seems to be declining.

The obvious first choice for an investor would be the finest quality Iranian weaves, including those with silk pile. Turkish and Caucasian rugs, when they're available, are also more likely to retain and increase their value, and there's a possibility that Romanian and Bulgarian rugs may also become better investments in the future—better, at least for the time being, than Indian and Pakistani rugs. (Don't forget, though, that while Indian and Pakistani rugs aren't particularly good as investments, they *are* good value for the money.) Chinese pieces, although they're extremely well made, are often very stylized, so there's less of a market for them. However, this may change as the Chinese adapt their designs to the demands of the marketplace.

Unfortunately, because of the vagaries of supply and demand, it's impossible to offer you a more precise prediction of what specific kinds of rugs, from which particular countries, will turn out to be the best investments among new Orientals. But despite this, there is one thing that you can be sure of. Barring an international financial calamity, it's certain that the prices of all rugs will keep on increasing. Most other markets have ups and downs, but the Oriental rug market has seen only a steady, continuous rise. For this reason alone, the time to buy an Oriental rug is *now*.

GLOSSARY OF TERMS

abrash Variations in the shade of a single color within a carpet, usually appearing in a horizontal line. Abrash can be caused when the weaver uses wool to which the dye has been unevenly applied, or uses wool from different dye lots. Even within the same dye lot, abrash can be caused by differences in the water used to rinse the dyed wool or by differences in the wool itself.

all-over A term used to describe a repeated pattern that covers the entire field of a rug. This type of pattern is usually woven without a central medallion.

acanthus A design motif consisting of large, segmented leaves that look like thistles. These are often seen in the capitals of Corinthian columns.

Anatolian A generic name applied to all rugs that come from the high plains of central Turkey.

antique The strict definition of an antique rug, which is still used by the United States Customs, requires that the rug be over a hundred years old. In reality, most rugs from the nineteenth century, even if they're less than a hundred years old, are now considered antiques. The term ''antique'' also refers to a type of chemical washing which gives an old look to a rug. This process is generally used on Chinese rugs that have been woven in the Peking design.

arabesque A design element consisting of complex, intertwining vines, tendrils, leaves, and flowers.

Aubusson A rug woven in France using the kilim, or slit-tapestry, technique. The term is also used to refer to the familiar design of these rugs, which generally features a floral medallion worked in pastel shades.

bag A small, square pile rug with a long kilim that folds back to form a compartment. Originally hung over the back of a pack animal.

border The band or stripe—or group of bands or stripes— around the edge of the rug that forms a frame to enclose the central field. The border stripes, which almost always are present on all four sides of the rug, are worked either in a single color or in various patterns.

boteh A classic design element from which the well-known paisley motif is derived. Also referred to as a pear, a leaf, a pine cone, or a palm.

Brailu A quality designation given to Romanian rugs that are woven on cotton foundations and contain 160,000 knots per square meter (105 knots per square inch).

Brasov A quality designation given to Romanian rugs that are woven on woolen foundations and contain 160,000 knots per square meter (105 knots per square inch).

broken border A border that's extended into the field rather than separated from it by straight lines. This type of border is usually much more closely related to the pattern in the field of the rug than other borders are. It's usually seen in rugs that are based on French designs.

Bucharesti A quality designation given to Romanian rugs that are woven on cotton foundations and contain 110,000 knots per square meter (72 knots per square inch).

cartoon The design of a rug, as it's represented on graph paper. Each block, or square represents a single knot in the pile.

cartouche A design element that faintly resembles a panel. The cartouche may be solid colored, or it may contain an inscription, a date, or another design.

Caucasian A generic name that refers to the geometric, boldly colored designs that were originally produced in the Caucasus Mountain region.

ceyrek The Turkish name for village rugs measuring approximately 4½ by 2¾ feet.

chemical wash A process in which a sheen is imparted to the pile of a carpet. This is produced not only through the action of the chemicals on the colors in the wool, but also by the chemicals' action in removing short, staple fibers that tend to absorb light.

chrome dyes Modern synthetic dyes that use potassium bichromate to create a bond between the dyestuff and the fiber.

cicim The traditional word for an Anatolian blanket made of several different bands of undyed kilim fabric that have been sewn together and embroidered. Also called a *djidjim*.

cloud band A design element, usually associated with Chinese rugs, which actually appears in floral patterns throughout the world. The figure resembles wispy clouds or the Greek letter omega.

corner A major design element in many carpets. Usually contains either a quarter section of the central medallion or some other distinct pattern.

covered   A term that describes how much of the central field of a particular rug is occupied by the design. A covered field is the opposite of an open field.

Crown   A prefix sometimes attached to the name of a traditional rug type or a trademarked rug name. This is often used to suggest a degree of quality, but it has no real significance.

density   A measure of the quality of the rug's construction that's determined by two factors: the number of knots and the height of the pile in a given area of the rug.

dhurrie   A flat-woven carpet made in India using the warp-sharing, kilim technique.

djidjim   See *cicim*.

double prayer rug   A rug with an arch at both ends of the field. See *mihrab, prayer rug*.

dozar   An Iranian term used for rugs that measure approximately 6½ by 4½ feet in area.

dragon   A design found in Chinese rugs that combines the characteristics of many beasts. This design is also seen in stylized form in carpets from other weaving areas.

drugget   A pileless carpet from India or the Balkan countries. Usually woven with goat hair, cotton, and jute.

elephant foot   See *gul*.

embossing   A technique used in finishing carpets in which feathered incisions are made in the pile where different colors meet.

Feraghan   A town in the Arak weaving district of Iran. The name is often used to describe rugs made using the Herati design.

field   The largest area of a carpet; the central portion that's enclosed by the borders.

foundation   The warps and wefts of a pile rug.

fringe   The continuation of the warp threads at each end of the carpet. Sometimes knotted or plaited.

fugitive dye   A darker color that has bled, or run, into an adjoining lighter color in the pile of a rug.

garden rug   A design in which the field of the rug is divided into squares or rectangles that contain plants and animals, or outdoor scenes.

Ghiordes   See *Turkish knot*. Also a classic style of Turkish rug (often a prayer rug) the design of which is characterized by narrow borders and abstractly drawn flowers.

gold washing   A process, usually seen in rugs from Afghanistan, in which the original red color of the pile is bleached out to shades of gold, coral, and amber after the weaving process has been completed.

ground   See *field*.

gul   A design element consisting of a squat polygon, usually arranged in rows and columns. At one time, each different gul represented a different tribal coat of arms.

guli hinnai   A repeating design consisting of rows of brightly colored, stemmed henna flowers.

hali (qali)   A Turkish word that means "carpet."

Harmon   A quality designation given to Romanian rugs that are woven on woolen foundations and contain 200,000 knots per square meter (130 knots per square inch).

hatchli   A design in which a large cross divides the field of the carpet into quarters. From the Armenian word for cross.

heddle   A horizontal rod or beam on a loom to which every other warp thread is attached. This creates a shed through which the weft threads are passed.

Herati   The most common repeating pattern in Persian rugs. Formed by a rosette surrounded by a diamond with small palmettes at its points and curving, tapered, serrated leaves that resemble fish along its sides.

Imperial   See *Crown.*

Indo-   A prefix used in combination with the name of a traditional rug type to identify India as the rug's country of origin.

jufti   A knot that's woven over more than the normal two warps. This reduces weaving time but yields a rug of inferior quality. Jufti knotting is usually done where the design of the rug incorporates large areas of a single color.

juval   The Turkish term for a bag or bag face that measures 6½ by 3¼ feet.

Kafkazi   A Turkish word meaning "Kazak." Now used by Pakistani weavers to describe their thin-pile, Caucasian-design rugs.

Kashmir   A rug-weaving district in the western Himalayas. The name has also been incorrectly used to describe the Soumak weaving technique.

kellegi   An Iranian term used for rugs measuring 10 to 12 by 5 to 6 feet. Formerly the headpiece in the traditional carpet arrangement of a Persian room.

kenareh   An Iranian term used to describe long runners.

kilim   A pileless carpet in which colored wefts form the face of the finished weaving. This term also refers to the pileless web sometimes found at either or both ends of a pile carpet.

line   A unit for measuring the quality of a rug, based on the number of pairs of warp threads in a given area of the carpet, usually one linear foot. The term ''line'' is also used to describe a border stripe that consists of a single row of knots.

loom   The frame on which warps are attached and kept rigid during the weaving of a rug.

luster   The sheen that's given to the surface of a carpet as a result of chemical washing.

Majestic   See *Crown*.

mat   A small rug that measures about 5 or 6 feet square.

Mauri   A name used either by itself or as a prefix to describe rugs worked in traditional Turkoman designs.

medallion   A single large design or a series of large designs that appear in the middle of a rug's field.

mihrab   The prayer arch of an Islamic mosque, as depicted in the field of a rug. Usually no larger than 6½ by 4½ feet.

Milcov   A quality designation given to Romanian rugs that are woven on a cotton foundation and contain 300,000 knots per square meter (195 knots per square inch).

millefleurs   A pattern in which small flowers are repeated throughout the field of the rug.

Minahani   A repeated pattern of diamonds formed by intersecting vines, with rosettes at the corners of the diamonds and in their centers.

mir   A repeating design of small botehs arranged in rows.

Moldava   A quality designation given to Romanian rugs that are woven with mercerized cotton pile and contain 200,000 knots per square meter (130 knots per square inch).

mordant   A chemical used to create a bond between the dyestuff and the fiber.

Mures   A quality designation given to Romanian rugs that are woven on cotton foundations and contain 200,000 knots per square meter (130 knots per square inch).

Mustaphi   Formerly a rug-weaving area in the Arak district of Iran. Today the name refers to a large-scale repeating design that features abstractly drawn flowers.

namase   An Iranian term used for rugs that measure around 4 by 2 feet.

namazlik   The Turkish name for a prayer rug.

numdah   A felted goat hair rug from Pakistan and India that's decorated with colorful designs embroidered in wool.

Olt   A quality designation given to Romanian rugs that are woven on cotton foundations and contain 250,000 knots per square meter (165 knots per square inch).

open field   A solid-colored ground, with or without a simple medallion and corner designs.

painted rug   A rug which has been dyed on the surface after the weaving has been completed. This process, often found in rugs from Arak (Sarouk, Lilihan), was intended to intensify certain colors which could not be produced in deep enough shades in the original pile yarns. The practice of painting rugs is much less common today than it once was.

Palace   See *Crown*.

palmette   A design element composed of a cross section of large, leafy, fan-shaped flowers. Usually multicolored.

panel   See *garden rug* and *cartouche*.

Persian knot   A knotting technique in which one end of the yarn is drawn up between two adjacent warp threads and the other end is drawn up on the outside of the pair. Also called an asymmetrical knot, or a Senneh knot.

pile   The surface of a carpet, formed by the cut ends of the knots that are tied onto the foundation.

Postavaro   A quality designation given to Romanian rugs that are woven on woolen foundations and contain 230,000 knots per square meter (150 knots per square inch).

prayer rug   A small rug featuring a prayer niche (mihrab) in the field design. Inspired by the architectural forms found in a mosque.

Princess   See *Crown*.

pushti   A Turkish term used for a mat or rug measuring approximately 3 by 2 feet.

qali   See *hali*.

repeated pattern   See *all-over*.

rosette   A design element composed of the symmetrical, head-on view of a flower. Usually round, with radiating petals.

Royal   See *Crown*.

runner   A very narrow rug. The length greatly exceeds the width.

Safavid   The ruling dynasty in Persia during the golden age of rugmaking from the sixteenth to eighteenth centuries. See *Shah Abbas.*

saff   See *saph.*

saph (saff)   A rug containing a number of adjacent prayer niches. Sometimes referred to as a family prayer rug. See *prayer rug, mihrab.*

Savonnerie   A hand-knotted, pastel-colored carpet made in France that's used as a model for many modern Indian and Persian rugs. The design features a floral medallion set on an open field, with broken borders.

seccade   A Turkish name for a village rug that measures approximately 6½ by 3¾ feet.

sedjade   An Iranian word for a rug measuring about 7 by 4 feet.

selvedge   The side edges of a rug that are formed by the continuous weft threads. The selvedges are sometimes wrapped in a separate process after the weaving is finished, either by overcasting or buttonholing. Note: the top and bottom edges of the rug form the fringe.

semi-antique   A rug that's neither antique nor modern. A rug made in a style that's no longer in production may be called a semi-antique even if it was woven relatively recently.

Senneh   A knotting technique; see *Persian knot.* Also the former name of a town in Iran where fine, single-wefted rugs were woven.

Seraband   A pattern in which rows and columns of botehs are repeated throughout the field of the rug. See *mir.*

Shah Abbas An intricate pattern frequently used in designs that cover the field of a rug. Consists of intertwining tendrils and vines with palmettes, rosettes, and, on occasion, vases and cloud bands. Named for the greatest patron of the arts during the golden age of Persian weaving. See *Safavid*.

shed The V-shaped separation of alternate warp threads on the loom, through which the wefts are passed.

shou A Chinese ideograph for the word happiness. Often seen in the patterns of Chinese carpets.

Soumak A flat-woven or pileless rug in which the pattern-forming yarns pass over either two or four warps and return under one or two warps, in contrast to the kilim method, which uses a basketweave technique.

spandrel The space between the arch of a prayer rug and the rectangular frame, or border, of the rug. See *prayer rug, double prayer rug*.

Spanish knot An unusual variation of the Turkish knot in which a knot is tied on every other single warp thread, with knotted warps alternating on each row.

Super See *Crown*.

torba A Turkoman bag measuring approximately 4 by 2½ feet.

Transylvania A quality designation given to Romanian rugs that are woven on woolen foundations and contain 121,000 knots per square meter (80 knots per square inch).

tree of life A design featuring a large tree that divides the field of the rug in half.

Turkibaff A rug made with Turkish knots.

Glossary of Terms

Turkish knot   A knotting technique in which the pile yarn is looped around two adjacent warp threads and then brought up between them. Also called a Ghiordes knot.

Turkoman   A generic name that refers to the geometric, repeating designs that were originally woven by nomadic tribes in central Asia.

tufting   A process in which the pattern-forming pile yarns are inserted into the foundation of the rug with the use of a handheld machine.

verneh   A geometrically designed, flat-woven rug made of narrow kilim strips that have been sewn together and brocaded.

warp   The foundation threads of a rug that are strung from the top to the bottom of a loom. In Oriental rugs, the knots are tied on the warp threads, which also form the fringes at the ends of the finished rug.

weft   The foundation threads of a rug that are strung across the width of a loom. These threads are passed through alternate warp threads after each row of knots is tied. They serve to secure the knots in place and also form part of the sides (selvedges) of the rug.

yastik   The Turkish term for a very small rug or pillow cover, measuring approximately 3¼ by 1½ feet.

zarcharak   An Iranian word for a rug that's about 4 by 2½ feet square.

zaronim   An Iranian term for a rug measuring approximately 5 by 3¼ feet.

Zel-i-Sultan   A style of rug that was once made in the Feraghan-Sarouk area of the Arak district of Iran. The term now refers to a repeating design made up of small vases of rose or red flowers.

205

ANNOTATED BIBLIOGRAPHY

Azadi, Siawosch, *Turkoman Carpets and the Ethnographic Significance of Their Ornaments*. Fishguard, Wales: The Crosby Press, 1975. $75, 128 pp.   This slim volume, filled with excellent color plates, is considered the definitive work on Turkoman carpets. Impressively researched, filled with interesting background information, the text covers the subject as thoroughly as possible. Of particular interest is the detailed discussion of the meaning and origin of the symbols used in Turkoman designs.

Edwards, A. Cecil, *The Persian Carpet*. Atlantic Highlands, New Jersey: Humanities Press, 1975 (text edition). $70, 384 pp.   Edwards' work, which was originally published in 1953, has long been considered one of the prime sources in the field of Persian carpets. In it you'll find a detailed description of rug production in the first half of the twentieth century, much of which remains valid for today's market. However, bear in mind the fact that most of the rugs featured in this book are now considered semi-antiques.

Eiland, Murray L., *Oriental Rugs: A Comprehensive Guide*. Boston: New York Graphic Society, 1976 (revised edition). $27.50, 214 pp.   A scholarly and comprehensive guide that includes interesting historical details, as well as a careful description of the weaving process itself. Eiland's primary concern is the identification of antique and semi-antique, rather than new, rugs.

Formenton, Fabian, *Oriental Rugs and Carpets*. New York: McGraw-Hill, 1972. $14.95, 251 pp.   Formenton's book is organized in the traditional way, according to weaving areas. His color plates are accompanied by a text that offers a wealth of anthropological and technical detail.

Gregorian, Arthur T., *Oriental Rugs and the Stories They Tell*. New York: Scribner's, 1975 (3rd edition). $30, 132 pp.   This brief but fascinating book describes the cultural backgrounds of the various rug-producing peoples. Included in the text are descriptions and illustrations of nineteenth- and twentieth-century rugs that are apt to be found in American collections.

Hawley, Walter A., *Oriental Rugs, Antique and Modern*. New York: Dover, 1970. $6, 320 pp.   This moderately priced paperback is an unabridged reproduction of Hawley's classic, which was originally published in 1913. Although most of the information on the availability of particular types of rugs is dated, the section on design remains valid and contains many fascinating details. This section is also very comprehensively illustrated.

Herbert, Janice Summers, *Oriental Rugs: The Illustrated Buyer's Guide*. New York: Macmillan, 1978. $16.95, 157 pp.   This recently published book makes fine reading for anyone interested in buying a new Oriental rug. Herbert includes a particularly interesting and well-illustrated description of the distinctions between hand-knotted and machinemade rugs.

Iten-Maritz, J., *Turkish Carpets*. New York: Kodansha, 1977. $50, 353 pp.   An informative and comprehensive study of this major rug-producing country. The material is arranged according to the geographic location in which the various rugs are produced. Features many fine illustrations of twentieth-century carpets.

Izmidlian, Georges, *Oriental Rugs and Carpets Today: How to Choose and Enjoy Them*. New York: Hippocrene, 1977. $8.95, 128 pp.   This guide, written by a London wholesaler, is primarily for the

British market, but it does have some helpful advice to follow when you're shopping for a rug. Izmidlian's very practical text offers a brief overview of the subject, along with some excellent color plates and a profusely illustrated and very comprehensive glossary.

Jacobsen, Charles W., *Checkpoints on How to Buy Oriental Rugs.* Rutland, Vermont: Tuttle, 1969. $17.50, 208 pp. Written in the author's inimitable style. The text contains some useful pointers on where and when to buy, what to look for, and objective criteria to use when you're comparing rugs.

Liebetrau, Preben, *Oriental Rugs in Colour.* New York: Macmillan, 1963. $6.95, 131 pp. A popular, reasonably priced manual. Liebetrau, a Danish rug dealer, provides a general survey of history, weaving techniques, and design, and then presents a series of color plates illustrating the most common rug types. Unfortunately, this material is now somewhat dated.

Lorenz, H.A., *A View of Chinese Rugs: From the 17th to the 20th Century.* London: Routledge & Kegan Paul, 1972. $57.95, 194 pp. Lorenz' book is considered the authoritative work on Chinese rugs. It features a comprehensive discussion of colors and patterns, as well as a detailed study of the origins and development of various symbols. The book is no longer in print, but it's well worth a look through the stacks at your local library.

Neff, Ivan, and Maggs, Carol, *Dictionary of Oriental Rugs.* London: AD Donker, 1977. $29.95, 238 pp. Neff and Maggs have divided their book in two sections. The first provides a comprehensive directory of terms and names associated with Oriental rugs; the second is composed of a series of color plates showing both the fronts and backs of different types of rugs, with accompanying texts describing how the various types can be identified according to their weaving techniques.

Petsopoulos, Yanni, *Kilims: Flat-Woven Tapestry Rugs.* New York: Rizzoli, 1979. $85, 394 pp. Petsopoulos presents solid general information on the forms, techniques, colors, and stylistic groupings of various types of kilim rugs made in Anatolia, the Caucasus, and Persia. The foundation of the book is his basic grouping of various types of kilims, and the aesthetic basis for understanding their design and construction. Profusely illustrated, with 400 plates.

Schlosser, Ignaz, *The Book of Rugs, Oriental and European*. New York: Bonanza Books, 1963. $25, 318 pp. Useful general information on rugs made on the Continent, as well as those from the traditional rug-producing countries. The book is no longer in print, but may be found at many libraries.

Schurmann, Ulrich, *Caucasian Rugs*. London: Allen & Unwin, 1964. $125, 360 pp. This magnificently illustrated book is the definitive work on Caucasian rugs. Although some of Schurmann's research hasn't been verified, his terminology has been adopted throughout the rug industry.

APPENDIXES

Appendix A
Plotting a Floor Plan

Before you set out in search of a rug, it makes sense to know exactly what size you need. An easy way to determine your options is to prepare a drawing of the room in which you plan to use the rug. The following grid (which may be scaled to your own needs) can be used for this purpose. Be sure to include the placement and dimensions of large pieces of furniture that are in the room (tables, sofas, beds, etc.), as well as architectural details (doors, windows, hearths, columns, etc.). Take the drawing with you when you go shopping, along with a paint sample of your wall color and a swatch of upholstery fabric, if possible. (You may wish to make a few photocopies of the grid sheet before using it.)

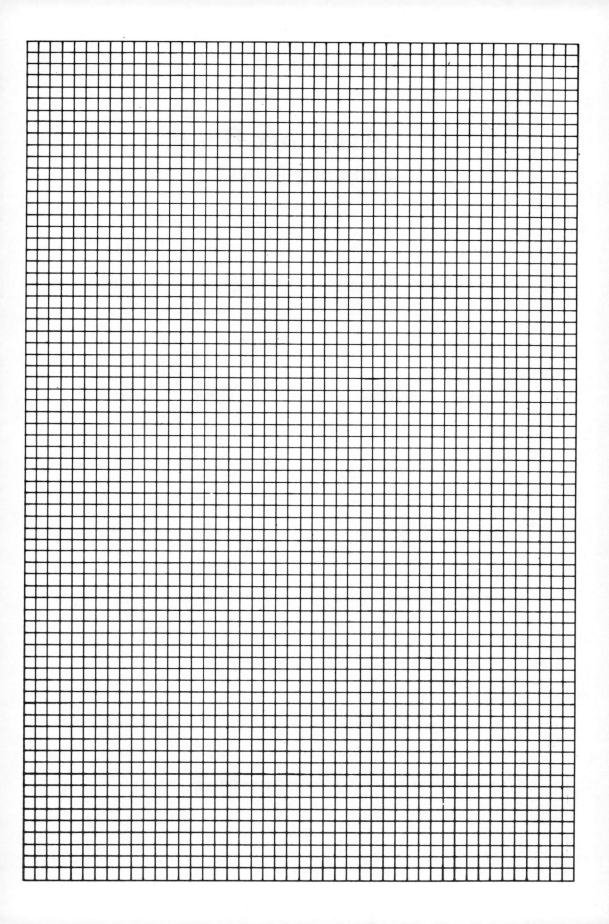

APPENDIX B
*Shopping Notes**

*Dealer*_____ *Date* _____

*Address*_____

_____

*Phone*_____ *Salesperson*_____

TYPE	COUNTRY OF ORIGIN	SIZE	COLOR & DESIGN	PRICE
_____	_____	_____	_____	_____
_____	_____	_____	_____	_____
_____	_____	_____	_____	_____
_____	_____	_____	_____	_____
_____	_____	_____	_____	_____

Additional comments (approval terms, trade-in policy, etc.):

_____

_____

_____

_____

*Photocopy this form and use it as a guide when shopping with various rug dealers.

APPENDIX C
A Permanent Record of Your Purchase

Whenever you buy a rug, make a photocopy of the following form, fill it out, and place it, along with a photograph of the rug, in a secure place, preferably a safe deposit box.

Place of purchase _____

Address _____

_____

Phone _____

Rug type _____

Size _____ *Purchase price* _____ *Date* _____

General description _____

_____

_____

_____

_____

Appraiser _____

Date _____ *Value* _____

Insurance agent / policy number _____

_____

Index

A

Abadeh, 147
abrash, 75, 85, 194
acanthus, 194
Afghan, 135, 147–148
Afghanistan rugs, 135–137.
  See also names of specific
  types.
Afshar, 148
Ahar, 148
Akhisar, 178
all-over design, 92–93, 194
Anatolian, 194
aniline dyes, 75, 85
animal designs, 91
animal hair, for pile, 74
antique, defined, 194–195
  semi-, defined, 203
antiquing, 194–195
appraisal, 188–189
arabesque, 195
Arak, 148–149
Ardebil, 149
asymmetrical knot, 69
Aubusson, 92–93, 195
  Chinese, 132
auctions, 81–82

B

bag, 95, 195
Bakhtiari, 150
Bakshaish, 177
Baluchi. See Belouch.
Basmakci, 150
beetles, carpet, 185
bedroom, rugs for, 112
Belouch, 136, 150–151
Bergama, 178
Beshir, 140–141, 151
Bibibaff, 150, 176
Bibicabad, 151–152
Bidjar, 152
Birjand, 177
Bokhara, 140–141, 152–153

Bokhara *(cont'd)*
  Pakistani, 127–128
  Tekke, 174
  Yomut, 176
Borchalou, 153
Bordchelu. See *Borchalou.*
border, 87, 88
  broken, 88, 195
  defined, 195
  design of, 92
boteh, 91, 195
Brailu, 139, 195
Brasov, 139, 195
broken border, 88, 195
Bucharesti, 139, 196
Bulgarian rugs, 143
buying. See also *sale(s).*
  floor plan for, 110–111
  rules for, 83
  sources for, 76–85

C

camel hair, for pile, 74
Canakkale, 178
carpet, defined, 21
carpet beetles, 185
cartoon, 29, 30, 196
cartouche, 196
catalog buying, 80
Caucasian, 140–141, 196
ceyrek, 196
chemical washing, 72–73, 196
Chi Chi, 178
Chinese rugs, 130–134. See also names of
  specific types.
  and Taiwanese rugs, comparative value of,
    142–143
  designs of, 92
  Indian copies of, 124
chrome dyes, 74–75, 85, 196
cicim, 196
cleaning, 182–184
  dealer's responsibility for, 106–107
  in manufacture, 72–73
clipping, 72
cloud band, 91, 196
color, 84–87
  and geographical area, 86
  choice of, guidelines for, 114

217

Index

Romanian rugs, 137–139. See also names of
  specific types.
rosette, 202
Royal. See *Crown.*
rug, defined, 21
  Oriental. See *Oriental rug(s).*
rugmaking, golden age of, 24, 116–117
  in Afghanistan, 135–137
  in China, 130–134
  in India, 123–127
  in Iran, 116–120
  in Pakistan, 127–130
  in Romania, 137–139
  in Soviet Union, 139–141
  in Spain, 141–142
  in Taiwan, 142–143
  in Turkey, 121–123
  minor areas of, 143
  present state of, 26–27
  steps in, 28–32, 65–75
runner, 203
Russian rugs, 139–141. See also names of
  specific types.

S

saddle bag, 95, 195
Safavid dynasty, 24, 116–117, 203
saff. See *saph.*
sale(s), auction, 81–82
  catalog, 80
  foreign, 83
  mail-order, 79–80
  private, 82–83
  wholesale, 79
Salor, 153, 179
saph, 93, 203
Saraband. See *Seraband.*
Sarab. See *Serab.*
Sarap. See *Serab.*
Sarouk, 170–171
Saruk. See *Sarouk.*
Saveh, 177
Savonnerie, 92–93, 203
sculpting, 133–134. See also *embossing.*
seccade, 203
secondary stripes, 88
sedjade, 203
Sehna. See *Senneh.*
sellers. See *dealers.*

selvedge, defined, 203
  inspection of, 104–105
semi-antique, defined, 203
Semnan, 178
Senna. See *Senneh.*
Senneh, 171, 203
Senneh knot, 68–70
Seraband, 170, 172, 203
Serab, 171–172
Serapi, 157, 178
Serrebend. See *Seraband.*
setting the foundation, 32, 65–66
Shah Abbas, 91, 204
shampooing, 183
shape, irregularities in, 102
shed, defined, 65, 204
  reversing of, 65–66
Shiraz, 172–173
Shirvan, 173
shou, 204
silk, for pile, 74
  for wefts, 74
Sinneh. See *Senneh.*
Sivas, 178
size(s), and geographical area, 96
  choice of, guidelines for, 97–98, 110–112
  custom, 96–97
  limitations on, 94–95
  standard, 96
  traditional, 96
slit tapestry, 66
snake design, 91
Soumak stitch, 67, 204
Soviet Union, rugmaking in, 139–141
spandrel, 204
Spanish knot, 70, 141–142, 204
Spanish rugs, 141–142. See also names of
  specific types.
Sparta. See *Isparta.*
sponge rubber padding, 182
spot removal, 184
stacking the warps, 66
stain removal, 184
stair runners, 112–113
storage, 185
stripe(s), border, design of, 92
  guard, 88
  secondary, 88
Sultanabad, 178
Super. See *Crown.*
symmetrical knot, 69

Index